MANAGING PEOPLE IN THE HOSPITALITY INDUSTRY

This is a book about being a successful manager in the complex hospitality industry. Approaching the subject in the context of personal development, it offers future managers essential knowledge and insight into the opportunities, the constraints, the problems and the solutions that face management at any level in the industry.

Structured in six parts, this comprehensive volume is not merely concerned with the social and psychological aspects of people management, but also with the economics of labour, including: labour costs, utilisation, labour market behaviour and pay. These aspects are conjoined in the book with the skills of people management to reflect the dynamics of real-life practice.

Combining theory and practice, *Managing People in the Hospitality Industry* offers a concise portrait of the industry at work and is essential reading for the hospitality managers of tomorrow.

Michael Riley is Professor Emeritus at the University of Surrey, UK.

Hospitality Essentials Series
Series Editor: Roy C. Wood, Faculty of Business and Law,
University of Northampton

Hotel Accommodation Management
Edited by Roy C. Wood

Strategic Questions in Food and Beverage Management
Roy C. Wood

Improving Sustainability in the Hospitality Industry
Frans Melissen and Lieke Sauer

Managing People in the Hospitality Industry
Michael Riley

For more information about this series, please visit: www.routledge.com/
Hospitality-Essentials-Series/book-series/RHE

MANAGING PEOPLE IN THE HOSPITALITY INDUSTRY

Michael Riley

LONDON AND NEW YORK

First published 2019
by Routledge
2 Park Square, Milton Park, Abingdon, Oxon OX14 4RN

and by Routledge
52 Vanderbilt Avenue, New York, NY 10017

Routledge is an imprint of the Taylor & Francis Group, an informa business

© 2019 Michael Riley

The right of Michael Riley to be identified as author of this work
has been asserted by him in accordance with sections 77 and 78 of
the Copyright, Designs and Patents Act 1988.

All rights reserved. No part of this book may be reprinted or reproduced
or utilised in any form or by any electronic, mechanical, or other means, now
known or hereafter invented, including photocopying and recording, or in
any information storage or retrieval system, without permission in writing
from the publishers.

Trademark notice: Product or corporate names may be trademarks or registered
trademarks, and are used only for identification and explanation without
intent to infringe.

British Library Cataloguing-in-Publication Data
A catalogue record for this book is available from the British Library

Library of Congress Cataloging-in-Publication Data
A catalog record has been requested for this book

ISBN: 978-1-138-29686-2 (hbk)
ISBN: 978-1-138-29688-6 (pbk)
ISBN: 978-1-315-09968-2 (ebk)

Typeset in Garamond
by Apex CoVantage, LLC

Printed and bound by CPI Group (UK) Ltd, Croydon, CR0 4YY

Contents

List of figures		vii
List of tables		viii
Preface		ix

PART I
Management judgement and decision-making | 1

1	Management judgement and decision-making	3
2	Personal and organisational knowledge	13

PART II
People at work | 23

3	The importance of a good start – the psychological contract	25
4	Motivation	32
5	Negative behaviour	46
6	Commitment, job satisfaction and empowerment	52
7	Group behaviour and teams	63
8	Understanding attitudes	73
9	Identity and diversity	81
10	Organisations and authority	86

CONTENTS

PART III
The economics of labour in hospitality   95

11 Economics of labour in hospitality   97

12 Hotel and catering labour markets   108

13 Throughput management – productivity   117

14 The measurement of labour turnover and stability   130

PART IV
Human resource management in practice   135

15 Administration – the necessary bureaucracy   137

16 Pay management   143

17 Appraisal   154

18 Recruitment and selection   160

19 Grievance and dispute management   174

PART V
The wider perspective   179

20 Developing Human Resource Management (HRM) strategies   181

21 Managing in an international environment   190

PART VI
Development and careers   197

22 Development and careers   199

Bibliography and further reading   203
Index   205

Figures

1.1 Handling uncertainty – it must be resolved	10
2.1 Type of knowledge	16
2.2 Embedded knowledge requirements	19
4.1 Expectancy theory	39
5.1 Dissonance and its resolution	49
7.1 Group process	67
7.2 Own-group and out-group	68
7.3 Action-centred leadership (J. Adair)	71
9.1 Multiple influences on personal identity	83
11.1 Supply curve for labour	101
12.1 Skill structure of hospitality units	111
12.2 Skill and mobility model	112
13.1 A short-term forecast of demand and labour supply	122
18.1 A sample hiring standard	162
18.2 Interview format	165
18.3 Selection interview information dilemma	165

Tables

10.1	Types of power	93
11.1	Job characteristics and market type	103
11.2	Dimension of internal labour markets	105
12.1	The occupational structure of hospitality establishments	110
13.1	Forecast and workload prediction	123
13.2	Estimating employment level from a forecast	124
13.3	Labour supply adjustment	125
13.4	Option for supply adjustment	126
13.5	An example of cross-substitutability of labour	127
14.1	Labour turnover and stability indices for nine hotels	133
18.1	Examples of general and episodic questions	169
18.2	Sample of culinary questionnaire	170
20.1	An overview of corporate HRM	182

Preface

Managing people is neither easy nor simple and there are no proven off-the-shelf recipes. It is for this reason that this book has placed managing people in the context of personal development; there is knowledge and skill that can be learned. This book is about being a successful manager in the hospitality industry, so, in essence, it is about your development as a manager in the context of a modern industry that is both international and business- orientated. The book is concerned to explain the management of human resources in hospitality, and in doing this it illustrates the opportunities, the constraints, the problems and the possible solutions that face management at any level in the industry. The author is an academic with many years of experience of managing in the industry, so the book is both academic and practical and, where appropriate, it uses theory to explain practice. The emphasis on personal development is to convince you that the knowledge you need to succeed as a manager can be developed. The book covers both the social psychological aspects of people management and the economics of labour. These aspects are conjoined because in real life they are inseparable. The book also offers some good practical techniques for human resource management and concludes by setting the task of managing people in an international context.

The book espouses important theories and concepts in each chapter then shows how these matter to hospitality management. The book assumes that the reader is a student of hospitality or a manager in the hospitality or tourism industries. The specifics of hospitality are accumulated throughout the book so that the reader has a comprehensive portrait of the industry at work. The book is in six distinct parts, which all have at their root the following broad learning objectives:

- to understand the complexity of managing people in hospitality;
- to understand the mental tasks of managers through the process of decision-making;
- to understand people at work and how theory is helpful to this task;
- to understand how the hospitality industry labour markets actually work;
- to understand that managers have to appreciate the breadth of organisational and industry knowledge;

PREFACE

- to understand how traditional hotel management sits with modern business practice.

Further reading

At the end of each chapter there will be a very specific paper or book chapter that extends and enhances the ideas within the text you have just read. Not all the articles are contemporary but they are there because they say something important and fundamental. Some of these papers are generic and some are about hospitality; either way they contain something important. The hope is these readings will offer an interesting trail to follow. One or two chapters which are without specific further reading attached are augmented by texts in the bibliography. A bibliography and additional further reading is located and the end of the book.

Structure of the book

Part I is called 'Management judgement and decision-making' and is from the perspective of the individual – you! It asks you to think about your decision-making and to reflect upon what knowledge is actually valuable to a manager. The rationale for this approach is that managing is a thinking task and needs to be taken seriously and reflected upon.

Part II is called 'People at work' and relates the theories of behaviour science to work in the industry. This section forms the essential theoretical background for managing people.

Part III is called 'The economics of labour in hospitality' and begins by highlighting those aspects of economics that are relevant to hospitality and then describes a model of skill, pay and mobility. The reader will be introduced gradually to a portrait of labour markets that explains the skill levels, pay distribution, mobility patterns and conditions of supply and demand.

Part IV is called 'Human resource management in practice' and features some of the necessary techniques of this function as they apply to hospitality.

Part V is called 'The wider perspective' and is more strategic, describing the international context in which hospitality HRM operates. The focus is on issues, modern business and careers.

Part VI is a single chapter called 'Development and careers' and hopes to convince the reader of the central platform of knowledge which a practising manager needs to forge a career in hospitality. It reiterates the 'big points' from the previous chapters.

There are twenty-two chapters in the book and each one will begin with a rational for its content which will be followed by some learning objectives which are there to guide you through the text.

PART 1
Management judgement and decision-making

CHAPTER

1 Management judgement and decision-making

In this chapter we are concerned with knowledge of the decision-making processes and how reflection on these can assist you to improve. We know something about decision processes and why they are important. They are at the heart of your personal development; as a leader/manager you will think and reflect on how you make decisions and take action. Experience just doesn't happen – you have to evaluate it: what works and what doesn't work and why. Your decision-making process will change over time. You will develop techniques which work for you – a personal style that carries authority and which you feel comfortable with when giving orders. Your decision-making will be influenced by your perception of your role and the organisation.

Chapter objectives

The principal objective of this chapter is to encourage you to reflect on your own personal way of making decisions and taking action. To achieve this you must understand and be mindful of these fundamentals:

- to appreciate the context of decision-making in hospitality;
- to understand the fundamental task of managers and mental tasks that flow from that;
- to understand that the act of judgement links information, knowledge, communication and action;
- to understand that the standard rational model of decision-making needs to be carefully interpreted;
- to understand that handling uncertainty is a distinguishing feature of individual performance.

Let's get straight to the heart of the matter; you will never have all the information you need to make a decision. You can Google-away a day and it still won't be enough or, worse still, it might even be too much and confuse. There will always be uncertainty and you have to handle it. That said, the question as to what constitutes good leadership can be addressed in many legitimate ways, but the resulting complexity can hide something obvious and

MANAGEMENT JUDGEMENT AND DECISION-MAKING

fundamental – that you need to make good decisions. The hospitality manager lives in a vibrant environment and has to constantly make contingent decisions; it is not something that can be avoided or postponed. What, then, constitutes a good decision?

There is an old saying in motivational practice that people go towards what they can see. Whilst true, it carries the corollary that someone has to paint the picture that inspires. Is that you? It should be because here is one big clue as to career success in hospitality management – being able to make your decisions clear and inspirational. Not easy at all! Yet the one thing you cannot be is indecisive. There is no magic wand to help nor any one-size-fits-all formula for being decisive and making good decisions, but it is worth remembering *that this ability can be developed and should be seen as part of your personal development*.Decision-making and, just as importantly, the communication of your judgement is at the heart of the personal development of a leader/manager. Your decision-making will change over time, but what will never change is that the response you get from those people you manage will, to a large part, be based on the quality of your decisions. Decisions are in fact active reflections of judgements and it is judgement that leads us to knowledge. So when we think about decision-making we must subsume it within the notion of judgement, which is dependent on knowledge and the idea that a decision has to be communicated. Communication is inseparable from the decision itself. We know three things about decisions:

1. *that they are always context specific* and therefore your judgement will be tempered by your understanding the situational, organisational and industry context. The circumstances and the broad setting are inseparable in your deliberation on what decision to make. Knowing how it all works is part of everyday life in a complex industry such as hospitality. Liking people and being good with people is fine but not enough. The message is clear; you have understand your industry to manage within it.
2. *that there is always time pressure*. The pressure from action is for a limited amount of information-gathering and a limited amount of alternatives evaluated. This pushes the decision-maker towards what they already know – prior beliefs about what works.
3. *that decisions have to be acceptable*. The individual manager is a sovereign thinker and self-determining agent but one who functions within a social organisation. The decision-maker has to process their judgement through the acceptability of outcomes to those who have to implement the decision and to colleagues.

The hospitality context

In the light of the above, it is now worth looking at decision-making in the context of operational management in the hospitality industry. The aim here is to outline the choices that face operational management in the short-term and in the long-term by analysing the dilemmas that they must confront. The notion of a dilemma always implies, and often combines, three particular properties: choice – which path to go down? Uncertainty – what are the paths and where do they lead? And, to make it harder for the decision-maker, possible conflict between the alternatives – the essence of a dilemma!

In looking at the dilemmas that face operational management, it is difficult to avoid two conclusions that might at first appear rather strange. Namely, that the problems of running an operation seem always to be there as if they were inherent in the very activity of managing hospitality and, perhaps more significantly, that they appear the same in units of different sizes, which only goes to reinforce the sense of permanence. This is not a counsel of 'there is nothing new' or one of 'managers do not solve problems' – on the contrary, there are new approaches including some technological solutions, and managers do solve their problems.However, managerial initiatives only solve the problems that stem from the fundamental dilemmas that are inherent in operations management. In a world of constant change it is easy to forget that many things remain constant.

It follows, therefore, that in understanding operational dilemmas we must seek out key managerial problems that require decisions and then identify the sources and level of uncertainty, the range of alternative solutions possible and the in-built conflicts that attach themselves to the problems. At one level the generic sources of the uncertainty are fairly obvious – the marketplace, competition and the human dimension. Some of the alternative solutions are equally conspicuous – to make or buy-in, to seek new markets or to stay loyal to the existing customers, to use full-time or part-time staff, to sub-contract. Similarly, it is relatively easy to see the sources of conflict within decisions – economic imperatives, of which profitability is central, versus sustainable quality. In production terms, there is, for example, the speed versus quality balance to be struck. This broad sweep analysis is important for perspective, but in operational terms what really matters is the detail but, equally, in looking at the detail it is important to remember the three properties that are invariably at work – uncertainty, competing alternatives and built-in conflicts.

Management in hospitality lives in a world dominated by two primary sources of uncertainty – variable consumer demand and the subjective evaluation, by the consumers, of the products and services they provide. It is from these twin pillars that many operational dilemmas ensue. A good place to start, therefore, might be with the consequences of uncertain demand. Given that hospitality operating units have a fixed capacity and that the products are perishable (that is – a room not sold or a restaurant seat not occupied cannot be resold), the goal of maximising occupancy is problematic. There are two components to this problem – the level of demand and the fluctuating nature of demand.

The appeal of the product and the level of demand

The economics of all hospitality units are based on throughput for which the key concept is the breakeven point. In a sense, achieving this over-rides almost everything. Given a degree of cost control, the solutions lie mainly within the realm of marketing, but marketing can only work from the product or service itself and here there are operational dilem-mas. There are three issues – how wide to pitch the appeal of the product, how much choice to offer and how to maximise the average spends. The decision to go for a wide range of market segments implies that the prod-uct has properties that will appeal to different consumers. For example, within the same range of disposable income might lie retired, middle-aged and youth markets, business and tourist markets, and local, national and international markets. This may be good for business, especially as they all seek the same satisfaction from the product, but it may not be so, in which case management have to work to make the same product satisfy different sets of expectations. If the latter is the case, the solution is to know which attributes of the product appeal to which markets – the dilemma is that there is a limit to how far a product can be altered to have multiple appeals to a differentiated market. Creating an image, which has multiple appeal and a reality that satisfies it is the point where operations and marketing meet. The alternative is for the product to be positioned in a way that it appeals to a specific market or small range of markets. In this case, it is more crucial for marketing to know what attributes would appeal to that market and then for operational manage-ment to design the product and service to meet that demand. What lies behind both cases is the argument that the less uncertainty there is for the customer, the more likely they are to consume.

The second issue relates directly to this problem of controlling uncer-tainty for customers.How much choice do we give customers? The ini-tial dilemma here is if wide choice is attractive. If wide choice is deemed to be an attractive attribute, then another dilemma follows, which is that wide choice leaves open the opportunity for products and service to be provided but not consumed. For example, a large range of dishes on a menu may entice the customers to dine, but if they choose narrowly, then the avoidance of waste becomes an economic issue and a managerial objective. In these circumstances, the ideal solution would be that eve-rything be cooked to order. The culinary expression à la carte has reso-nance with the modern production management technique of 'just in time management', where products are not made until they are sold. The problem is that the very attractions of cuisine work against cooking to order – some dishes require long cooking times. The solutions lie in the technology of food production, storage and regeneration. The alternative to wide choice is specialisation – offering to produce a small variety at a controlled level of quality. This would be more productive but may reduce the size of the market. In a sense, the width of choice dilemma is about appeal versus productivity. One concept, which straddles both these ideas, is that of branding, whereby although the choices on offer can be wide or narrow, specifying the choices within the overall concept of the brand reduces some of the uncertainty for the customer. It does not remove the issue of range of choice versus productivity but takes it into the identity of the product and by so doing handles the attractiveness issue separately from the production issues. The uncertainty of consumer choice presents problems for management, but such issues are subsumed by the major one of the fluctuating nature of overall demand.

Fluctuating demand

At the macro level it is easy to see a pattern of seasonality in consumer demand, but for operational purposes the key issues lie in the handling of short-term fluctuations in demand. In the context of accommodation, the key decision is how many rooms are there left to sell that day. The guiding stars are the 'house count' for that night, advanced reservations and scheduled checkouts for that day. It is a decision based on some information, and its consequences are the degree of alacrity with which sales strategies are pursued. However, uncertainty intervenes in the form of:

- how many advance reservations for that day will actually show up;
- how many 'chance' customers will turn up without reservations;
- how many customers who said they would check-out that day decide not to.

The only solid fact is the number of rooms occupied. Management's solution to this problem is to take the three unknown variables and one know variable and model them into an equation which uses historical data and forms the basis of a 'rolling forecast'.

If to the problem of maximising occupancy is added the issue of maximising revenue, then the equation takes on another set of dimensions. One way of filling up rooms is to alter the price. This has led to a sophisticated form of pricing (or discounting) known as yield management. In this scheme of things prices are altered at a rate that reflects the state of demand and rooms vacant ratio. This is merely a formalised way of expressing the inherent dilemma of the need to fill the house versus the need to maximise revenue. Selling cheap might fill the house but reduce revenue and profits. The arrival of an unexpected coach party only willing to pay at a large discount for numbers may give the duty manager a headache.

Of course, pricing is one of many competition mechanisms, and it is competition that lies at the heart of uncertainty in management. The key questions are: who is the competition? And, how do we compete? Market information is never perfect, but the best information we have is, on the one hand, on the performance of units in our market category (similarly positioned) and, on the other, whatever we can glean from our own customers. There are two basic dilemmas here: firstly, do we compete on price and therefore logically on discount in line with competitors or on other dimensions? If it is on qualitative dimensions, should we be negative about the competition or simply emphasise the merits of our unit? Marketing always speaks of 'differentiating the product' even within the same market – but how?

Irrespective of how fluctuating demand is handled, there are consequences for the supply side of operations. In order to maintain profitability, the unit needs to adjust supplies in line with fluctuating demand. The hardest part of this dilemma surrounds labour costs. If demand is fluctuating, then that means a degree of flexibility of labour supply. Most advocates of quality in services suggest that employment continuity is a key element. The dilemma here is simply profitability versus continuity of service in circumstances where the demand for labour varies. Resolution of this dilemma is difficult and is the driving force of human resource management in hospitality. In hospitality, the permanent and the temporary, the skilled and the unskilled, the high tech and low tech all have to live together. So you have the dilemma of managing diversity and workforce instability. The dilemma for human resource management is whether to manage the whole workforce as if it were skilled and permanent or as unskilled and temporary. Economics goes for the latter, whilst the consumer demands for quality advocates the former. As a manager it is your call!

Let's pause for a moment from dilemmas to think about efficiency. Although the hospitality business is usually referred to as a 'service industry', any of its units contain both service, distribution and production functions. As all processes have priorities, this sometimes leads to what are known as technological or work process conflicts. For example, in a hotel, reception wants the rooms ready now! Whereas housekeeping wants them clean – it is a speed versus quality dilemma. Similarly, good service is never slow, so the waiter wants the food now and the chef wants it to be just right – these are the in-built conflicts which often have to be managed.

One approach to efficiency which cuts across all these issues is that of seeing the organisation in terms of processes – systems that serve the goals of efficiency and customer service. It is about flows of customers and flows of materials and their timing. It is about conceptualising products and services and delivering them in ways that are efficient in terms of resources and inviting to customers. There are two dilemmas here: first, that system design must begin with a conceptualisation of the service or product which has the confidence of the market. To start designing a process from a concept surrounded by uncertainty is to make the whole organisation uncertain as to its own efficiency – the basic dilemma of process engineering. It is right for management to assert their designs on the product rather than be simply reactive to the market, but there are risks. The second dilemma is that system design places all its emphasis on the service to the customer and makes resource provision subservient to that. This carries the tendency to favour out-sourcing and de-skilling because the wider implications of change are excluded from the vision. Again, as a manager it is your call.

From the above description of the context of hospitality, it should be clear that the contingent nature of activity means that handling uncertainty under time pressure is an essential part of decision-making. It should also be clear that there is plenty of scope for initiative. Decisions, in this context, carry two probabilities:

- RISK – the probability that a particular outcome will result from a given decision;
- UNCERTAINTY – when the problem is not clearly defined, and the probability of alternative outcomes cannot be estimated or calculated.

So what to do?

It is very easy to argue that business is rational and that leaders, entrepreneurs and managers make their decisions on the rational principle of evaluating every option to gain maximum utility. It must be true because all the economic textbooks tell us so! To be fair to them, they do acknowledge the imperfect distribution of information. What this means in reality is that all agents making decisions do so with limited knowledge and within the context of bounded rationality. A shorthand version of bounded rationality would be that within an organisation the thinking of each manager would be bounded by the goals, norms and values of the organisation as experienced within a proscribed role. What the manager does not know is known by others and this creates a mutual dependency within the social group which is the organisation. We are dependent on each other's knowledge to be effective. Nevertheless the rational model of decision-making which suggests both probabilities can be handled by pure rationality is valid.

- All information relevant will be gathered and evaluated.
- All possible outcomes will have their consequences evaluated.
- All solutions will be compared and preferences ranked.
- An optimal or best sub-optimal solution will form the basis of a decision ...

If we look more closely at uncertainty, we can see that it has implications for communication to others and for the individual's understanding of the situation about which they have to decide.

- Incompleteness – not enough information.
- Indeterminacy – means and ends cannot be estimated.
- Irrelevance – what information is applicable and what is not.
- Incommensurability – there is no basis for comparison.

However, the significance of uncertainty of any type is that the manager will have to make a judgement and consequently a decision despite being faced with uncertainty. Figure 1.1 illustrates how judgement needs to capture whatever form of uncertainty is present.

As a manager you are the author of the action which follows from your decision. At its most simplified and fundamental, a manager's role is about conceiving and describing a task (either discrete or continuous) to be achieved and designing an appropriate organisational form in which it can be controlled and achieved. If it ends in an action, where does this conceiving start?

A decision has to be born; it has to start somewhere. Where? It begins with the manager's perception of the environment and the sensing of an

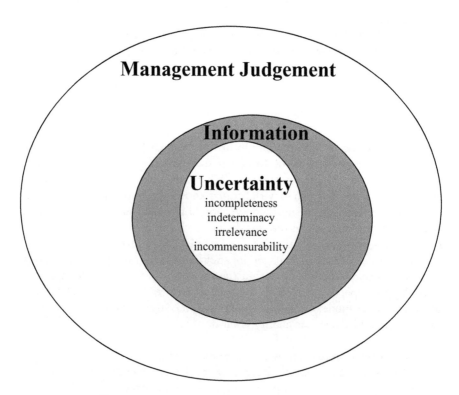

Figure 1.1 Handling uncertainty – it must be resolved

opportunity or a problem. Here is a crucial stage on the road to decision because how we conceive a problem or an opportunity will determine how we decide upon it. Often we initially assess a problem or an opportunity in terms of 'what causes that?' If we make a mistake such as misattributing the cause we may mislead ourselves into taking the wrong decision. We describe the problem or opportunity to ourselves before we evaluate it; this requires some analysis or synthesis. This process may require some decisions itself; do we use our prior knowledge? Do we go looking for information? Is there a need for creativity and intuition? These are not abstract concepts.Everyone can think creatively, and 'gut feelings' are not to be dismissed as irrational. Then after evaluation we must decide whether or not to make a decision! If we say yes, then we get to the stage where we can make a decision. Does decision imply action? In other words, once you commit to a decision are you automatically on a path to action? Having made a decision we next need to decide to act. Once committed to action there is the problem of communicating your decision, and here we loop backwards to your original conception of the problem or opportunity. If we described the problem clearly to ourselves, then we can describe the proscribed action and solution to others.

Below is the sequence of managerial thinking and decision-making – the decision process.

- Sense a problem or opportunity.
- Conceive the problem or opportunity into a rough definition.
- Frame in your mind the problem or opportunity.
- Analyse the problem or opportunity – what knowledge applies?
- Value the problem or opportunity – make a judgement.
- Decide to act.
- Make a decision.
- Analyse the possible consequences of the decision – will it work?
- Decide on a communication strategy.
- Take action.

Notice that judgement and knowledge precede decision-making and that communication is part of the decision process and not an afterthought.

The immediacy of decisions in hospitality

Most forms of analysis of managerial work always combine the seriousness of the decisions being made – in terms of consequences of error – against the time pressure under which those decisions are made. In the hospitality industry, there is a sense of immediacy brought about by contingent demand and perishable sales. Whether it is deciding how hard to push today's unsold rooms or ordering tomorrow's fresh ingredients against an uncertain expectation of demand, the pressure comes from the short time span. What is more, these contingent decisions are continuous. If, to this flow, we add the huge range of areas of decision-making and add the fact that calculations will invariably be necessary, then the

MANAGEMENT JUDGEMENT AND DECISION-MAKING

dilemmas of decision-making in hospitality become clear – it is a constant, complex and basically tactical process. The pressure from action works against the search for information; what time pressure argues is for a limited amount of information-gathering and a limited amount of alternatives evaluated – and therefore encourages a dependence of *prior beliefs about what works*.

Earlier we said that decisions have to be acceptable, so in the next chapter we examine this aspect of decision-making in the context of not only knowledge but the idea of prior beliefs about 'what works'.

Further reading

Baron, R.A. (1998) 'Cognitive mechanisms in entrepreneurship: why and when entrepreneurs think differently than other people', *Journal of Business Venturing*, 13, 4: 275–294.

Why read this? If you have any experience of managing and making decisions, you will recognise the thought processes clearly described in this very interesting paper.

CHAPTER

2 Personal and organisational knowledge

In the previous chapter on the process of decision-making, the emphasis was on judgement and how that was founded on knowledge. You know how to cook, you know how to deal with guests and you can fold a napkin in a dozen attractive ways – is it enough? It helps and it is certainly important, but you will need more. The issue with hospitality jobs is that, on the ground, they are very specific, intense and small scale. When you are working in a restaurant or at a hotel front desk there is enough to concentrate on without thinking of the bigger picture. Yet your personal development and career depend on accumulating a much wider and deeper pool of knowledge than you are currently using. Hospitality is, in many respects, traditional, but like any other modern industry, it is now part of the information society and uses knowledge and data techniques of modern business. The skills associated with this must therefore be part of modern hospitality education. It is for these reasons that you are encouraged in this chapter to think about knowledge and how it is applied and what knowledge you value. We introduce two concepts: firstly, human capital, which is simply the sum of your personal knowledge; and secondly, knowledge as belief in the form of pragmatism and the idea that managers always carry in their heads a notion of 'what works and what does not'.

Chapter objectives

- to appreciate that there are ways of seeing our own knowledge;
- to introduce the concept of bounded rationality;
- to understand how managerial knowledge can be categorised to show to what purpose it can be applied;
- to understand how prior knowledge impacts upon decision-making.

The hospitality context

Like any traditional industry, hospitality is built upon a foundation of practical knowledge, some of which amounts to skilled craftsmanship. It is one of the traditions of the industry that managers must know how to cook, serve and clean in order to run a hospitality establishment. It is a valid tradition. This tradition internalises vast amounts of practical knowledge and grafts on to it an emotional attachment. It is also useful in daily life. How can you guide the work of others if you cannot do the work yourself? How can you define and judge quality if you cannot yourself produce it? How can you correct a mistake if you do not know how it came about? This thinking extends beyond understanding jobs to work systems and routines. You have to understand how kitchen and restaurant interact; how reception and housekeeping interact. This thinking can be summed up by asking how far management should understand the jobs and systems they are managing. The tradition in hospitality is that they should understand the practical tasks and systems. The human argument is simple: if you have done the operative jobs, then you know how much effort they require and the frustrations that occur and the motivations intrinsic to the job. This is the understand-your-workforce argument. It enhances your personal authority with your staff through them respecting your skills.

This argument is not totally undercut by modern business practice, but change has brought new knowledge into the industry – that is, what might be called pure managerial knowledge: computing, marketing, finance, human resource management. Staff respect you because you have managerial knowledge. What this represents is a disconnection between those who serve customers in various ways and the management and business of the organisation. The business can be run by knowledge of targets and ratios, forecasts and formalised processes that require no hands-on knowledge. What is interesting is that, although there is attrition between them, both new and traditional knowledge appear to need each other and co-exist together in the modern world of hospitality. Technology has introduced tighter control and granted the consumer greater power, but delivery is, for the most part, dependent on traditional skills. It is observable that the higher the class of establishment the closer the two approaches come together. This is a mixed message for aspiring managers but one which is best accommodated by recognising that both are necessary to a career. What is clear is that when looked at in terms of knowledge, the hospitality industry requires manual skills, timing skills, data manipulation skills, social skills and organising abilities, but what is unusual about this array is that they can, to a degree, be found in all jobs. The appellation unskilled has to be seen in this context.

Ways of seeing knowledge: three perspectives

We do not often think about our knowledge but it is worth doing so and setting it in its social context. At any moment we not aware of all our knowledge; we simply become conscious of it when we need it or when we deliberately call it up from memory. Much of our knowledge is contained in actions. You ride a bike

PERSONAL AND ORGANISATIONAL KNOWLEDGE   15

but you cannot explain how this knowledge was obtained except by reference to experience. This process applies to decision-making with important implications. Three perspectives on knowledge are helpful to unravelling those implications:

- that we have limits to our knowledge;
- that knowledge is something that carries value;
- that knowledge is accumulated in a social context.

We must acknowledge that we all have limits to our knowledge. The notion of bounded rationality captures this idea. It is commonly applied to the analysis of managerial behaviour and organisation analysis. Put simply, it is acknowledgement that we are all limited and the boundaries of our knowledge are, to an extent, commanded by our organisational roles. Again, to a degree, our thinking becomes encompassed by the limits of our organisational role. The common idiom 'thinking out of the box' is, in a way, an attempt to escape the bounds of our rationality. Bounded rationality can be characterised by:

- a limited capacity to handle information, and we can suffer from overload;
- sources of information that are constrained by our role in the organisation;
- the boundaries of our role becoming the boundaries of our thinking;
- mental short-cuts taken to avoid stress, and therefore we are subject to biases.

The second important perspective is that of valuing knowledge. We accept that some knowledge is internalised and tacit and often contained in habitual action. By contrast some knowledge requires exposition for it to be useful. More importantly, we need to look at knowledge in terms of whether the individual has a firm commitment to the truth of that knowledge or whether, without emotional commitment, the knowledge is simply assumed to be useful (secular). *Some of our knowledge we consciously value.* We do so for lots of reasons: it is useful; we had to make sacrifices to learn it; we found it hard to learn and many more. Some knowledge we simply take for granted and assume it is useful. Figure 2.1 lays out a setting for this form of analysis.

The importance of Figure 2.1 lies in the influence of the top left quadrant because it will contain ideas about what works. The significance of this cannot be understated for managers in a world of constant change. The danger is always that if we think we know what works we don't go looking for new knowledge. Prior knowledge is both necessary and useful but can also be problematic. The importance of prior knowledge comes from the fact that managers have to get things done! And, they need to feel competent. What better way than to use knowledge that they know will apply.

- Not all prior knowledge is a matter of conscious belief; there is knowledge to which the individual gives a degree of commitment (I know it will/will not work) and knowledge which is secular (taken for granted).
- Some knowledge is embedded in action (I always do it this way).
- Successful action and prior beliefs give a sense of competence.

MANAGEMENT JUDGEMENT AND DECISION-MAKING

	Belief	Secular
Explicit knowledge	Advocated belief based on prior knowledge	Assumed to work without question
Implicit or Tacit knowledge	Habitual practice	Unconscious, Taken for granted

Figure 2.1 Type of knowledge

The value of using prior knowledge is fairly obvious, and in a traditional industry like hospitality the manager may be on safe ground. However, the dangers need to be evaluated. Bounded rationality and valued prior knowledge can work together to create 'mind-sets' – that is, fixed ways of thinking that may be biased against the actual circumstances and, more importantly, act as a deterrent to look for new knowledge.

A typical mind-set might consist of:

- accepted ways of doing things (I know what works);
- what productivity is dependent upon (harder work/more technology);
- assumptions about how the industry works (industrial recipes – that is, the ways things are commonly done in the industry);
- assumptions about classification of consumers – who they are; where they come from;
- assumptions about what kind of people come to work in the industry;
- assumptions about what motivates people who work in the industry;
- what personal success is dependent on.

All these things are perfectly legitimate and indeed are necessary to proper functioning as a manager and to building a career, but what about new knowledge? What about looking at matters in an innovative way? Here is where the sovereignty of the individual really counts – you don't have to go along with the conventional wisdom of 'this is how we do things around here'. It is a choice. The idea that we might need new knowledge leads us to our third perspective – that there is knowledge embedded in a context which needs to be learnt if decisions are to be made that affect it.

It is one thing to accept that the individual manager is a sovereign thinker and self-determining agent but it is also necessary to see that that individual functions within a social organisation. Hospitality units are all social organisations in which collective knowledge is embedded which everyone must learn for the organisation to function. The mental task of the individual is to integrate their personal knowledge with that emanating from the circumstances as well as from the organisation.

What makes collective knowledge personal is that organisational activities, cultural signs and routines convey internalised principles and a rationale which has the effect of being accepted as personal knowledge by individuals; e.g. the ethos that the guest is always right becomes a guiding principle of the manager even in circumstances when it is inaccurate. Similarly, good service can be many things but not slow; which infects production routines. In this way, the organisational culture which develops becomes, for the individual, the realm of possible actions and, in effect, signals the hegemony of effective action over knowledge. It is 'action' which provides the nature of connectivity between the person and the organisation because it is through the individual's 'appreciation' of the context in terms of their prospects for action. In other words, knowing what you can do, how far you can go and the effects on the context is founded on your understanding of the organisation's culture.And it is 'being 'effective' that introduces the notion of pragmatism. The limits of human agency are shown as the personal limits of such appreciation; it is what managers believe to be possible that connects them to the organisation and its collective knowledge. This implies an active overlap and connectivity between the accumulated human capital of the individual and that of the knowledge embedded in the organisation, with both forms of knowledge being open to change and internalisation. If organisational knowledge is absorbed into personal knowledge to the extent that it invades decision rationality, then it becomes a form of active applied management knowledge. What, then, is applied management knowledge? First, we must think about how we see our own knowledge.

To reiterate, it is helpful for managers to see their knowledge in terms of its limits, what is personally valued and also to be aware that knowledge is collective and that using prior knowledge, whilst useful, can be limiting. If new knowledge is to be sought and action is to be taken, then serious thinking (cognitive effort) will be required and time compression handled (not everything can be Googled – you need to think).

What is management knowledge?

Management knowledge has been described as a cake that can be sliced many ways. It is not easy to quantify, yet some analysis would be helpful to actually managing. The place to start is the organisation. Although managers work in

MANAGEMENT JUDGEMENT AND DECISION-MAKING

social environments, through consent they are essentially sovereign decision-makers – individuals with their own motives, preferences and beliefs. They do not get up every morning and remake their conceptions of the organisation they work in, nor do they suddenly become aware of the pressure on them to get something done. You as a manager will have ready-made conceptions of how things work, what you are good at and how imperatives need to be met. In other words, prior knowledge impacts upon current circumstance, but, that said, we are still left with the question as to what management knowledge actually is. In addressing this question, scholars have sensibly used the organisational setting to categorise knowledge in a way which starts with a situation and then broadens to the widest possible scenario.

The listing below is a compilation of how academic research analyses organisational and management knowledge. It starts with knowledge needed for the smallest interaction then grows through the organisation to end in the broad setting of the organisation itself in its environment.

- *Situated knowledge*. The knowledge that is embedded in the situation. This is how the subject describes the problem/decision/solution.
- *Component organisational knowledge*. This is knowledge of the organisation's micro-processes and procedures.
- *Architectural organisational knowledge*. Knowledge of culture, norms and politics. Knowledge of the distribution of power.
- *Contextual knowledge*. Broader than architectural knowledge, this is knowledge of the broad market and economic scenario in which the situation under scrutiny is placed.
- *Technical knowledge*. How the subject understands the technological process they are managing.
- *Technical managerial knowledge*. This is subjective knowledge of managerial functions; e.g. marketing, accounting, HRM etc. and business models and process models.
- *Managerial change knowledge*. Knowledge used to manipulate, change and control the situation for strategic purposes.

Why is this categorisation important to you? It is important because you need to realise that handling a situation involves wider knowledge than that which appears, and, furthermore, it should make you realise that just as a career is more than a job, knowledge requirements are more than you need for a particular role. Knowing the big picture as well as the small one is the basis of career development.

Figure 2.2 expresses the relationship between the categories. Knowledge is embedded simultaneously in the context, the organisation and the situation.

These categories are not abstractions. Two examples might be useful:

> You approach a guest in your hotel coffee shop who insists he wants a dish that is not on the menu. You know that the guest was turned away

PERSONAL AND ORGANISATIONAL KNOWLEDGE

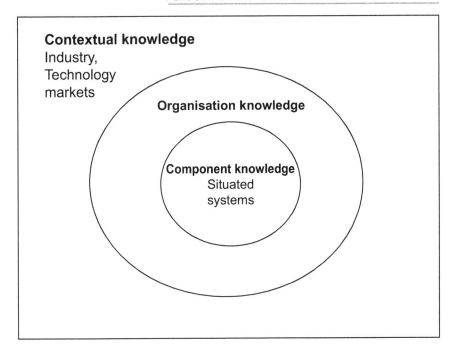

Figure 2.2 Embedded knowledge requirements

from the hotel's fine dining room because he was wearing shorts. The dish he is asking for is on the fine dining menu and the request is resentful (situational knowledge). You know the dish takes a long time to cook and that the coffee shop kitchen cannot make it (technical knowledge). You know that there is not a procedure for transferring hot food between the two kitchens as they are far apart. There would be disruption and an account issue (component knowledge). You know that the chef in the fine dining restaurant will not like the request and may object (architectural knowledge). The ethos of 'the guest is always right' hangs over the situation. However, you know that the dish is on the room service menu, which offers two possible solutions – persuade the guest that he would enjoy the dish in his room or use the transfer systems of room service to get the dish to the coffee shop without upsetting the chef (improvising around component knowledge). You make a note to charge the fine dining room price.

A customer on the phone demands an explanation as to why his altered booking has been met by the computer telling him the hotel is full and rejects his request for a three night stay. Originally he booked the first three nights of the month, then circumstances changed and he wanted to start his stay from the second of the month. Difficult to explain, but you have the component and routine knowledge about rolling forecasts

MANAGEMENT JUDGEMENT AND DECISION-MAKING

and social skills to explain how that works. You have the contextual knowledge to know that other hotels have the same system and possibly the knowledge that the city is not likely to be overbooked for that period. Armed with all this knowledge you have to plate and assist the customer. Do you suggest he tries again at a date nearer his departure date? Good luck.

What is management knowledge for?

You might think the answer is obvious – to enable you to get things done. Whilst true, it is worth reflecting that when your knowledge is applied through a decision it has some wider implications. No one wants to feel incompetent; therefore, your knowledge has to be demonstrably acceptable to others. To get anything done you don't just have to be competent – you need authority and you need for your decisions to have the consent of your peers and your workforce. Feeling competent, feeling secure in your authority and knowing that your group accepts your decision is the foundation of managing, and to a large extent this is based on other people's perceptions of your knowledge. We can then ask the question of how others judge your knowledge. The answer that comes back is likely to be 'through your decisions'. Here we have basic criteria for a good decision – it achieves its goal, it maintains your authority and it enhances your standing within your peer group. Basic but not enough.

The decision that carries your knowledge behind it has to be communicated. In a sense, a decision is about a description of the future – a mental vision of what you want to happen – what ought to happen. Going on the old adage that people go towards what they can see, if you can paint a picture of what outcomes you expect from your decision, then the likelihood of success is increased. It is a skill that can be developed.

Knowledge and innovation

In this chapter we have asked you to look at your own knowledge from three perspectives; to accept that your knowledge is bounded and therefore you need to expand your knowledge horizon; to realise that you value your knowledge differential and that that can lead to staid thinking and to a reluctance to seek new knowledge. There is one further dimension to knowledge that needs to be emphasised; that of sharing.

In our modern world it is absolutely necessary to innovation and to productivity that knowledge is exchanged. If people are inclined to declare their own knowledge in collaboration processes, then the outcome is likely to be new knowledge. This is the primary assumption of modern industrial thinking on innovation. It sounds like a good idea. However, if we recall our second perspective on knowledge, we see the potential problem of individuals' valuing some of their knowledge. Being committed to an area of knowledge may lead an individual to be possessive and territorial about that knowledge and be reluctant to share it. Given the importance of innovation, this is a managerial problem to be overcome. The vehicle for exchanging knowledge is reciprocity – giving in order to receive. This process lies at the heart of knowledge exchange collaboration. How active this process is is a matter of organisational culture.

Further reading

Baldwin, T.T., Pierce, J.R., Joines, R.C. and Farouk, S. (2011) 'The elusiveness of applied management knowledge: a critical challenge to management educators', *Academy of Management Learning and Education*, 10, 4: 583–605.

Why read this? This is basically academics scratching their heads trying to pin down what knowledge managers actually use. Despite their well-focused arguments, the target remains slippery. You get closer with the literature on organisational knowledge. The following paper picks up the drift of that literature and is a possible starting point: Chua, A. (2002) 'Taxonomy of organisational knowledge', *Singapore Management Review*, 24, 2: 69–76.

PART

II People at work

CHAPTER

3 The importance of a good start – the psychological contract

The aim of this chapter is for you to understand the nature of the management-worker relationship at its deepest level – the psychological contract. All relationships are based on unspoken assumptions, and at work that means assumptions about effort and reward and discipline and obedience: these issues lie deep but are always there. It is the layer that sits beneath motivation.

Chapter objectives

- to look at how the contract is formed;
- to understand the imprecise nature of the contract;
- to understand the covert nature of the contract;
- to understand how it differs from other explicit behavioural characteristics;
- to understand why management behaviour is always symbolic.

Almost everyone at some time has been surprised by an action by someone they thought they knew well – a close friend perhaps; 'that's not like them', 'that's out of character', are the kind of sentiments that follow. Yet the possibility exists that whatever our friend has done may be perfectly in character; it is only that our assumptions and expectations of them were wrong. All relationships have a taken-for-granted element to them. Things are not said – just understood to be so. The manager–worker relationship is like any other in this respect. Here we meet the 'psychological contract' and our friend from the first chapter – uncertainty.

The moment at an employment interview when the manager says 'start Monday' and the applicant says 'OK' is the moment when a relationship begins between a manager and a worker. From that moment on it becomes 'necessary' for each to have an opinion of the other. From that moment, each will influence the other's behaviour. Of course they are not equal, but nevertheless, each will affect the other's behaviour. As soon as the 'OK' is spoken, a psychological contract has been made which will change as the relationship develops but will last until one of them leaves.

PEOPLE AT WORK

The psychological contract usually referred to in behavioural science as the labour contract (note nothing to do with a legal employment contract) has two principal dimensions, which are:

1. effort – reward;
2. obedience – discipline.

The so-called effort-bargain and authority relations. How much effort do I put in for the expected reward? Which orders do I obey? How conditional is my willingness? How much discipline will I accept? These are the trade-offs and balances that form the heart of the contract – they are universal, but they exist for the most part in the realm of private thought rather than explicit behaviour. To see the importance of this, it is perhaps best to start at the beginning.

The original bargain is struck at the selection interview. The interviewer tries to assess the capacity of the interviewee in terms of effort and general willingness. The applicant's past record and references help in this process. The interviewee is trying to assess what is going to be required of them in terms of effort and obedience and whether or not it is worth the reward being offered. Both are really fishing and dealing in imprecise quantities. The agreement they finally make is, at that 'start Monday' point, very imprecise. Like anything which is imprecise, it is open to misinterpretation and is, as any agreement, potentially unstable. What keeps a psychological contract stable is the mutuality of the assumptions that lie behind it. If the amount of effort expected by the interviewer is the same as that anticipated by the interviewee, then that part of their relationship is stable. If they aren't the same, it is potentially unstable. This does not mean that it will necessarily lead to manifest conflict, because assumptions can be adjusted.

Suppose on Monday morning the worker finds the job harder than they anticipated but the manager less severe than expected. Similarly, the manager finds the worker less skilled and slower than they thought but seems more willing than they expected. It could lead to conflict, but it could simply be a case of adjusted assumptions on both sides. If the latter occurs, then what both have done has simultaneously and secretly adjusted their contract. They will go on adjusting expectations of each other as long as the relationship exists.

At this point, it is worth taking a rain check. Surely the role of human resource management in the selection process is to make everything explicit and precise? True, but it can never entirely succeed. In other words, the labour contract is always and everywhere, but to a varying degree, imprecise. To understand this, it is necessary to look again at what is being exchanged in the initial bargain. On the one hand, the employer is buying an unspecified potential and the employee is taking on an indeterminate amount of work. Good interviewing practice, job descriptions, previous experience of the same work and clear references can all help to make the assumptions of the parties more precise and mutual, but a job description cannot describe what

THE IMPORTANCE OF A GOOD START   27

effort will be required and therefore at the point of agreement even the tangible wage offered becomes subjectively evaluated. This is why, despite good human resource management practice, the agreement is always imprecise.

The nature of the job and the precision of the psychological contract

There are, however, degrees of imprecision which are determined by the nature of the technological process in which the job exists. In other words, some jobs make for very imprecise labour contracts, while other jobs attract more precise contracts, and the determinant of both is the nature of the job itself and how far management can apply formal controls. To illustrate this, it is helpful to contrast two jobs of widely differing technological mode. Suppose we have a job of pencil sharpener. A person sits at a lathe all day and picks up a pencil, runs the end across the lathe and places it in a box. Management could do a pretty good description of this simple task. They would specify the number to be sharpened per hour, the tolerances of the point and the number of breakages allowed. All this could be discussed at the selection interview to make things explicit. Contrast this with the job of a waiter. All the usual conditions such as hours of work, shift times etc. can be specified. The person is supposed to look smart and give good service. While it is possible to specify smartness, it is much harder to say what good service is. It is possible to lay down specific routines for the customer-service interaction, but the only person who can justify whether or not it is good is the guest. Management don't have the same degree of control.

What is being said here is that different jobs imply a different form of managing the people who do those jobs. Where the job allows management to measure the output precisely they will use formal controls, but where the output standards can only be specified subjectively other forms of managerial control become necessary.

With care and caution and with respect to generalisation, it is suggested that automated mass production industry work produces fairly precise labour contracts with tight formal management control, but service industries contain many jobs where very imprecise labour contracts exist and consequently more informal control processes are needed. It follows that labour management in manufacturing and in service industries is a different task. The argument here is that the more imprecision the greater will be the significance of the labour contract to the manager–worker relationship. What this actually means, is that more of the relationship will be based on assumptions and unspoken understanding rather than overt control measures.

A more nuanced view of the psychological contract argues that there are two types of contract: one which emphasises the extrinsic explicit elements of the contract without accounting much for intrinsic qualities of workers. Called transactional contracts they are more common in organisations with strong formal control systems. They are characterised by lack of trust and

28 PEOPLE AT WORK

greater resistance to change. By contrast, relational psychological contracts stress interdependence of the organisation and level of social exchange. They invite trust between the employer and the individual. It is important to understand that both these 'types' exist with a single contract simultaneously. It is a matter of emphasis.

The covert side of the manager–worker relationship

One of the traps that managers so often fall into is to use the satisfaction-dissatisfaction frame of reference as the principal method of interpreting employee behaviour. It is important, but it is not the sole frame of reference available. There are other ways of seeing.

What the notion of the labour contract tells us is that as the relationship is based on unspoken assumptions, much of what is so important is actually secret. The nature of these assumptions can only become manifest by being triggered by some behavioural event. For example, suppose that A, B and C work for you all with apparent satisfaction, then A leaves for a better job and you give A's job to B. Your relationship with C may well have been based on two incorrect assumptions. C may always have thought that he would get A's job if she left. You never intended to give it to C but to B. Only now can you and C know that your assumptions were never mutual and that, despite years of satisfaction, your contract was always unstable. Conflict may ensue. Another example, this time on the obedience-discipline dimension: suppose four people work together and one day the manager is unusually severe on one member of staff. Either intentionally or not, such action may signal to that employee and to the other employees that their future expectations of discipline may have to change.

This little example may be a trivial incident in daily life, but it illustrates three things. First, that whether they intend it or not, all managerial behaviour may be symbolic. Second, that symbolic communication impacts directly on the psychological contract, and third, that labour contracts are not simply individual; they can be interrelated with others. Each action by managers is judged against the currently held assumptions.

The following statements can be made now in respect of how managers and workers relate to each other.

- A relationship exists at a level of unspoken understandings and assumptions, as it were, below any consideration of satisfaction or manifest behaviour.
- The true nature of the psychological contract remains secret unless triggered by some event which questions an assumption held by either partner.
- The two dimensions of the contract can be traded off.
- Stability may sometimes be achieved by illicit means amounting to collusion.
- The scope for assumptions is determined by the nature of the job.

Hospitality psychological contracts and bureaucracy

In many respects, it is a frightening thought that all managerial behaviour sends signals – yet it is true. All behaviour communicates, but it is only symbolic where matters are not explicit. It is in areas of ambiguity that symbols play such a large part.

The hospitality industry is full of such ambiguity, with lots of jobs where the output is subjectively defined. What this means is that if you unintentionally pass a crumpled tablecloth in the restaurant you may be sending a message that you don't care! What you do and what you do not do speak directly to your workers by helping them to reinterpret their contracts with you. What is at stake here is your authority.

In conditions where standards are subjective, managers always try to overcome this subjectivity by standardisation, checklists and other aids which make what is required more specific. In other words, they try to improve formal methods of control. The problem is that these can never be totally successful. What the hospitality manager has to realise is that the effective weapons are personal and demonstrable – that is, example and vigilance with the objective of achieving a shared value with the employees as to what constitutes 'good' in the various circumstances of the operation are effective controls. It is a trust relationship. This relationship between the nature of a job and how management can control it leads to an important issue for the industry – control versus personal service.

In a bureaucracy, if your problem does not fit the remit of the person you approach, you will simply be passed on until either you find someone whose remit embraces your problem or you are left in high dudgeon. Hospitality services are not natural bureaucracies. The concept of personal service is about being flexible enough to respond to whatever problem a guest brings to the desk. To make this response, the employee's job must be defined in wide scope and that means a problem for management because the greater the scope of an employee's job the harder it becomes to exert control. Here is a dilemma and issue for management: if I want customers to have personal service, how much control can I exert before I stifle the initiative essential to personal service?

The first law of control is to make whatever it is controllable. Managers with responsibility for a particular area of activity will want to make matters within that area controllable. This is inevitably a process of standardisation involving putting constraints on the scope of jobs. Thus, management will try to define the job and reinforce standards by such devices as procedure manuals, training, reports and incentives. Technology allows management more and more opportunity to develop formal controls. This is a natural and correct process, yet it brings with it certain problems. It is a question of role expectations. Management have expectations, but the guest may have different expectations. The incumbents themselves will also have expectations and will interpret their role under pressure from both managers and guests. The approach of marketing to this problem would be to suggest that a 'level of

PEOPLE AT WORK

service' can be defined and in this way customers' expectation manipulated. This is only true up to a point. Customers have a way of not conforming to artificial limitations. The real alternative to personal service is self-service, but once roles exist that deal with people, it becomes difficult to limit the demands on those roles without incurring a reputation for poor service. It is a question of priorities. There are four natural pressures on job priorities:

1. to do what is required of you by the control system (in other words, give priority to what management will see);
2. to do what you are naturally good at or find cosy in the job;
3. to do what you really like in the job; *And for service employees:*
4. to do what the customers think is important.

The first three dynamic pressures take place in all jobs, but the fourth, exclusive to personal service workers, can often be a countervailing pressure to the demands of management. If you want personal service, and that is an important qualification, then the danger is of exerting too much control.

The formation of a contract and its importance

Scholarship in this area suggests the following phases of contract formation (see further reading).

- Pre-employment – the initial expectations of the employee form through reputational sources the organisation and occupations.
- The selection interview of two-way communication involving promise exchanges between employer and prospective employee during the recruiting process.
- Early socialisation – promise exchanges continue, with both parties actively continuing their search for information about one another through multiple sources.
- Later experiences – the promise exchange and search for information processes slow down as the employee is no longer considered new. There may be changes to the psychological contract introduced at this stage.
- Evaluation – the existing psychological contract is evaluated and possibly revised, and it is determined whether revision is needed. Incentives and costs of change impact revision.

The psychological contract is the smallest unit of analysis in understanding the manager–worker relationship. It lies beneath those psychological entities such as motivation and identity that have more conspicuous behavioural consequences. The contract is essentially covert until, that is, it is broken by one party or the other and no adjustment is made. What is important for you to understand is that all your employees have a psychological contract with you as indeed you do with your superior and with the organisation. If we accept that hospitality is becoming, through information technology, more bureaucratic, then it is worth asking how imprecise psychological contracts in this industry are. The more formal control exerted the more precise the contract becomes, yet quality standards might well be laid down in manuals but are judged subjectively. What is good service has to be demonstrated so that norms of behaviour are understood at the level of the contract – that is, assumed or taken for granted. There remains a strong element of normative control in hospitality whereby personal qualities and leadership have a direct effect.

Further reading

Rousseau, D.M. (2001) 'Schema, promise and mutuality: the building blocks of the psychological contract', *Journal of Occupational and Organizational Psychology*, 74: 511–541.

Why read this? This is one of many papers by this academic on the psychological contract, and it offers finer detail on the components of a contract and how it can be manipulated by both sides.

CHAPTER

4 Motivation

In this chapter we take a selective look at a topic which is very personal to managers – motivation. It is not uncommon to hear managers express the view that they put 'willingness', often meaning 'the right attitude', above skill and experience. All a bit unrealistic, but it is understandable because motivating others is not an easy task. Theories abound, but here we look critically at a select few that may have a wide practical significance. The theories of Maslow and Herzberg are well known to the point of being taken for granted or even being superfluous to management thought. Both are worth looking at more closely because when dissected they represent a rationale for the modern practice of teamwork.

Chapter objectives

- to appreciate the context of hospitality work;
- to understand the psychological needs approach to motivation;
- to comprehend the range of functions of motivation;
- to be aware that integration in the wider society affects motivation.

The hospitality context

An outside view of the industry might regard relative low pay, high labour mobility and the extent of immigrant labour together with a range of jobs that are either low or semi-skilled as evidence that managers face problems in terms of motivation. However, if the perspective is turned around, then enormous diversity and ease of learning jobs and thus access to earnings might be seen in a positive light. Hospitality is a social activity which attracts individuals who feel at ease in such environments. It can be bureaucratic but rarely predictable or regimented, and such assets can be appreciated.

A large majority of people who work in the industry are unskilled and therefore have a wide range of unskilled and probably mundane jobs to choose from. Yet they tend to stay in the hospitality industry, often

MOTIVATION   33

moving from place to place and often in and out of work, but by and large staying inside the wide confines of the industry. If they stay, there must be something in it; some basis of satisfaction.

Ask most people who seek a career in the industry why they do and they usually reply that they like working with people. Not a bad sentiment, but the implication behind it is that people means variety. The unpredictability of people together with the fluctuating nature of business demand creates a variety in work which is appreciated. Above all, however, is the fact that no job, no matter how mundane, is regimented. Even the dishwasher does not have the iron rigidity of the factory production line. There is a strong 'not factory' theme sitting in this area between job choice and motivation.

Unlike unskilled work in a factory, people have a degree of autonomy in their work, and we know that all theories of motivation speak of autonomy and control as a need to be satisfied. The point about mundane work in the hotel and catering industry is that it at least has the potential to be personalised. The attractiveness of unskilled hotel and catering work could be summarised as follows:

- convenient;
- easy to learn;
- has variety;
- grants autonomy;
- it is not a factory;
- you meet people.

So we are left with a conundrum: are the reasons why people come into hospitality the same attributes that motivate them at work? How do the attractive attributes play out action on the job? It is a hard question to answer, but what we do know is that surveys reveal high levels of job satisfaction even when pay is low. This is supported by the fact that although workers change employer regularly they tend to stay in the industry. In many industries satisfaction comes from having an end product. Hospitality has similar sources such as finished dishes. People get attached to things they have contributed to. What appears to happen in hospitality is that employees construct their own end product – that is, 'the satisfied customer'. There is a satisfaction to handling complexity and diversity which is what dealing with people amounts to. What is more, the social atmosphere and amenable working circumstances ameliorate the wealth gap between the server and the served. The reflection of a good life falls on both. One clue comes from Chapter 3, in that given the informality of imprecise psychological contracts that seem to be prevalent, the key factor in motivation is the behaviour of managers – their leadership.

This is the context in which we need to think about motivation.

Thinking about motivation

What gets us up in the morning – habit, routine, a sense of purpose? We make promises to do things and promises to decide things. Some of these intentions we fulfil; others we don't – why? Some people get more done than others: some set goals while others drift along; some can't get started; others can't be stopped. We are in the realms of motivation. Look at any group of people performing the same task and you will be obliged to conclude that some perform better than others. Such individual differences are often most marked with wide discrepancies between the best and the worst. This can be true even when selection has been careful and abilities assessed as uniform. If you look at any team sport, you see differences between players that cannot be explained by differences in natural ability, training and experience. There is another quality present. That quality is called motivation.

It is the very conspicuousness of individual differences that has led to motivation taking up a central position in management thinking and has led to a primary focus on performance. Seeing differences in performance as attributed to motivation has made management interested in influencing motivation in order to increase performance and in trying to select on the basis of identified motivation. Not surprisingly, therefore, management is interested in 'what motivates' and in using the answer to actually alter employee behaviour. Hotel and catering management has a real investment in motivation because most of its jobs require input where effort and personal character actually matter.

As one might imagine with something so important, theories abound. These theories fall into two broad categories: those about what motivates and those about the process of motivation – how it works. What most theories assume is that the best way to describe motivation is as an inner drive – some kind of decision mechanism which incorporates the will so that things aren't just decided upon but acted upon as well. What will become apparent is that there is a huge element of chance in motivating others. This is the message the theories tell us when the content and process are taken together – it's not an exact science ... Before asking questions about motivation and how to motivate, it is worth pausing to ask the all-important question: what are you motivating them for?

- To work harder?
- To be flexible about the job?
- To be loyal employees?
- To be committed employees?
- To learn new skills?
- To be part of a group?
- To abandon old skills?

Because motivation is always associated with performance, it is easy to forget that there are wider implications and wider applications of motivational strategies.

What motivates?

If two managers are left alone for a minute they will talk shop. After five minutes of sharing problems they will end up talking about motivation. What is more, the conversation will turn into a debate about whether money or job satisfaction motivates! This is a legitimate argument, but it is flawed. Maybe they are not alternatives; maybe both motivate, maybe neither motivate, but above all it is simply too generalised. Motivation has to be debated at a much more detailed level. A spot of theory.

Maslow

A very influential writer, Maslow's theory is based on the idea of human 'needs'. We have, he argues, physiological and psychological needs, and these needs are motivations when they are unsatisfied.

Maslow categorises human needs as follows:

- a need for self-actualisation (personal growth);
- a need for self-esteem;
- a need to belong and be loved;
- a need for safety and security;
- a need for food, drink, health, sleep (physiological need).

He argues that these needs emerge as motivations in the hierarchy as listed above, so that as the need below is satisfied, the next need emerges as a motivation capable of being fulfilled. This puts a premium on the higher needs because they are more open-ended and don't have an obvious finite limit. When you have eaten you have eaten; if you have a house you have a house; if your friends love you they love you, and too much praise can inflate the need for self-esteem, but personal growth has no obvious limits, although there must be some. It is this last notion that is so supportive to the advocates of job satisfaction. If people can grow at work, then as this need can never be satisfied it will always be a motivator. To do justice to Maslow, he does recognise there is some overlap in his hierarchy and that self-actualisation may have limits.

If we pick up on this possible overlap in his hierarchy a trail emerges which offers an explanation for a very modern form of motivation – the need to belong. Modern psychology has pursued the idea that people behave in what might be called identity-sensitive ways. In other words, Maslow's middle ranking 'need' becomes the platform for motivation. Ideas about group motivation and organisational commitment stem from this base.

Maslow's theory belongs to a humanistic school of thought which is optimistic in its view of human life and which is concerned with human potential. This brand of psychology focuses on what individuals are capable of and how they can realise their potential. Maslow created a theory of motivation in life not just in work. The fact that this theory has been so widely acknowledged in the world of work could be because it represents a humanistic justification for the job satisfaction movement in the face of the realities of so much

36 PEOPLE AT WORK

boring, mundane and menial work. If human beings are growth-seeking, potential-realising animals, then industry should not stultify this process – so the argument goes. The interest of management in Maslow's thinking is that the idea of 'needs' which can be fulfilled offers a target and a direction to the application of stimuli like money, interesting tasks or recognition. This unfortunately carries with it an unfortunate blight and that is that in trying to stimulate satisfaction managers tend to see motivation solely in terms of satisfaction and dissatisfaction and to see them as one continuous dimension. It is a matter of degree, the argument goes.

Herzberg

Seeing motivation in terms of a continuous dimension of satisfaction or dissatisfaction has the effect of suggesting that all facets of the work situation have the capability of being both satisfiers or dissatisfiers and therefore of being motivators. Not so, suggests Herzberg. Usually known as the two-factor theory, he argues that the work situation can be divided into dissatisfiers – elements that cause dissatisfaction but which when satisfied don't motivate – that he calls hygiene factors. Alternatively, there are satisfiers – that is, elements of the work which when satisfied actually motivate.

Note what he is saying here. Elements which satisfy and those which dissatisfy are not opposites. Elements such as conditions of work, supervision, pay and physical conditions can cause dissatisfaction and need to be attended to, but they do not motivate people to work harder. Elements that do that are the work itself, responsibility, recognition, achievement and advancement. By separating satisfiers from dissatisfiers he creates a zone of neutrality so that an individual's feelings can go from neutral to satisfaction and from neutral to dissatisfaction.

The unique contribution of Herzberg is in breaking the mould of one continuous dimension and at least introducing the idea of neutrality, which also opens up the possibility that we may be indifferent to certain aspects of work. Herzberg is, however, firmly in the job satisfaction camp. Note that his motivations are very much to do with recognition needs and growth needs.

It could be argued that all this human potential stuff fades when put against the moral simplicity of having to earn a living. This imperative argument underpins the 'pay as the only real motivator' school of thought. It is all a bit too simplistic. The arguments against the job satisfaction advocates don't actually need an alternative source of motivation and should be taken on their own. There are two broad arguments, which are, first, that there appears to be no great call for job satisfaction in that a lot of people do fairly mundane and boring work without conspicuous dissent. The second argument is that, however one might feel about human potential, much work simply cannot be organised to meet human potential needs. Dishwashing and room cleaning cannot be constructed other than for what they are – mundane work. However, the detective in you will have noticed that as alibis these broad arguments don't add up. There is no possibility of reconstructing the work

MOTIVATION 37

to make it interesting – true, many people must be abstracted out and feel like robots – but the very lack of dissent suggests most people have endlessly subtle adaption systems which can turn moronic work into something at least worth possessing, if not even cherishing. Here, then, is the dilemma of job satisfaction – the range of elements from which satisfaction can be gained extends beyond the normal list of jobs itself to pay, boss, work group, organisation, working conditions, achievement, advancement etc. The experience of retired people and the unemployed shows not just that work itself makes people valuable to themselves but that individuals 'latch on to' an array of elements, some of which might seem strange to the outside observer – some of which are known only to the incumbent of the job. If managers are seriously interested in tapping job satisfaction, the message is that it is a matter of detail. First find your satisfiers. One interesting example of the damage which can be caused by concentrating on work as the source of job satisfaction is the neglect of the power of the actual finished product or service to motivate. Previously, it had always been assumed that only craftsmen like chefs could derive any satisfaction of this kind because of the pride in their skills and achievement. It was, to some, astonishing that people who contributed a fragment, or only indirectly, to a product or service could find the result satisfying. This example also suggests that a sense of purpose might be heavily implicated in satisfaction.

The problem with theories based on satisfaction of needs is that sometimes we come across people who appear to be denying themselves fulfilment. Altruism, self-sacrificing behaviour, even self-destructive behaviour don't, at least, appear to be need-satisfaction activities – yet they might be? A theoretical framework which might help here is known as self-theory. The argument here is that we construct a subjective world, giving everything meaning in relation to the self.

Snyder and Williams

One of the problems of need theories is that while it may be obvious why we need food, drink and security, it is not obvious why we need recognition, advancement and growth, and this they do not explain. We all possess a unique view of the world and a unique view of ourselves. How we see the environment and ourselves in it becomes the essence of our individuality. We develop ways of seeing the environment which enable us to understand everything we see, and like a scientist we devise ways of predicting and controlling our world. We are not new every morning; we awake with knowledge, experience, a mental filing system for information and, above all, an identity.

The essence of yourself needs to develop but also needs to be maintained in a stable way. It's this maintenance function that is, for self-theory, the overriding need. Needs emerge because they maintain our conception of ourselves. People who see themselves as slim adjust their physiological needs. People who are not sure of their ability seek recognition. It is the image of the self

PEOPLE AT WORK

which is regulating the emergence of needs. It is easy to envisage that in the world of work an essential branch of our self-identity would be our occupational identity.

Fundamentally, what self-theory is saying is that it is our need to define ourselves that regulates our needs. In management terms this might be considered a further complication.

Perhaps it would be appropriate to conclude the discussion of what motivates by considering the case of Japanese organisations, who answer the question by saying everything does – *as long as it all makes coherent sense!* Western writers have concentrated on particular aspects of Japanese management such as quality circles and culture but have neglected the point that everything about employment is deliberate. In other words, every aspect of the individual environment is planned in a coherent way. The approach embraces needs theory and attempts to influence the self-concept by designing an environment that tells a coherent story. *The debate about what aspects of employment motivate may well hide a truth that they all do when held together.*

How does motivation work?

The simplest way to see the process of motivation is to see it as a stimulus-response mechanism. The individual perceives a particular stimulus, say, interesting work or pay and responds by working harder. Managers manipulate the stimuli in order to change the behaviour. It is not, alas, as simple as this. When we look at the process, it is easy to see how needs theories and self-theory work together through the medium of perception.

Ask any group of people to do a job for a reward and they all react in a different way. Not only does motivation vary between individuals but they respond differently to the same stimulus. This offers us a clue that the relationship between the content and process may explain the actual differences between people that we see.

Expectancy theory

Expectancy theory attempts to explain how a stimulus is turned into motivation or, put more simply, how a reward produces an enhanced performance. At the heart of the theory is something referred to as 'E'. What 'E' stands for is a wider definition of the drive of motivation. Think of as many words as you can that are similar to 'effort': energy, enthusiasm, expenditure, excitement. They all infer a 'drive' of some kind – motivation. How is the 'E' to be activated? The theory suggests a number of simultaneous stages:

1. the strength of the need is felt;
2. the expectancy that 'E' will produce a particular result;
3. the result will reduce the need.

What is being said here is that a person has, and recognises that they have, a particular need. This need will have a certain intensity or strength to it. Management ask for more effort in return for a particular reward. The person then assesses that by expending more 'E' it will produce the reward and that this reward will satisfy their original need. To put it more simply – the outcome is desired, and the effort is expected to produce this desired outcome. An example would be helpful. A banquet salesperson is wondering whether or not to make a few more sales calls. The additional sales will lead to a bonus (stimulus). The salesperson is aware that they could do with the money (the need). The expectancy is that by making more calls (effort) more sales will ensue (performance) and that the bonus will be forthcoming. However, everything in this calculus is dependent upon the attractiveness of the bonus. Will the bonus reduce the need? This aspect of attractiveness of the reward is often referred to as the valence of the reward. If the bonus was trivial it would reduce the motivation force considerably. Figure 4.1 illustrates the theory.

A query, a question and a useful reminder stem from expectancy theory. The query is over whether people are always conscious of their needs and are as calculating and rational as the theory implies. The question that arises is where do the expectations themselves come from? On what basis do we estimate that our 'E' will produce the required performance and get the reward? Previous experience of ourselves in similar circumstances and previous management behaviour would seem to be our only guide. This makes consistency

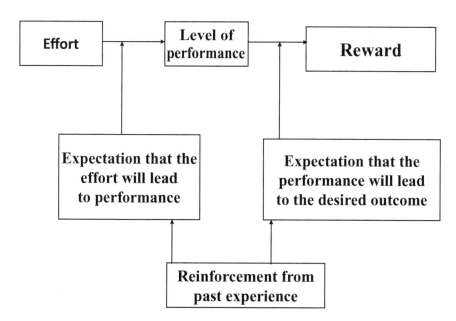

Figure 4.1 Expectancy theory

PEOPLE AT WORK

in evaluating performance a key area of managerial behaviour. The useful reminder which this theory flags up is that to respond to a stimulus, however subjectively, the individual must perceive it clearly, and this puts a premium on unambiguous communication.

So far the process of motivation has been seen entirely in terms of stimulus-response confined within the manager–worker relationship. Yet another powerful influence on our level of effort is our feeling of fairness and equity towards other people. Social comparisons are inevitable in a workplace, and it would be unimaginable that they would not influence behaviour.

Equity theory

Possibly the most readily understandable psychological process, equity is about feelings of guilt, anxiety, frustration, envy or psychological discomfort, engendered by comparisons with others – a common enough human process. At work, the focus is on rewards, effort and investment. People will strive to restore a sense of equity when inequity is perceived. It is this restoring process that alters behaviour. It is based on a ratio between inputs and outputs – the self and the compared other each having a ratio. Equity theory assumes that:

- people will modify their behaviour by the envious comparisons they make;
- the comparisons are based on assumptions rather than facts;
- there is a comparison matrix: my pay their pay, my effort their effort, my investment their investment.

What is important here is that this comparison is trading in perceptions; very little may be visible or factual. Effort is usually fairly conspicuous, but other outcomes and inputs, especially for the compared other, are likely to be guessed. When inequity is felt, the person will either take action to achieve equity or alter their perceptions in some way.

The problem with equity theory is that the only avenue for rectifying inequity is altering effort. This is easy to say but not so easy to do. Ability plays a part here. Everybody has a natural pace to the way they work which is not easily and consistently altered. Try walking abnormally slowly for a while! It may be better seen as an explanatory theory of relationships between people and of grievances rather than as a theory of behaviour modification. But, make no mistake; inequity is a powerful feeling which can create negative behaviour.

So far, the focus has been on motivation to increase performance, and the assumption has been made that motives can be found at work and that management can, within certain limits, influence motivation. Hold on. *People don't come to work as a blank sponge.*

It is all too easy for managers to overlook the fact that what motivates at work may originate outside work and that there may be some limitations on their ability to motivate, yet this must be true. Maslow's need theory, for example, does not specify that need satisfaction can only take place in the workplace. It must be accepted that some of our need and part of our self-identity comes from home, family, social life and other aspects of non-work life. The argument here is that to understand motivation it is necessary to broaden the perspective beyond work.

So far we have looked only at motivation in relation to performance, but what makes us perform may be related to other questions about work. There may be a link between:

- why we work;
- why we do a particular job;
- why we work for a particular organisation;
- why we give a certain level of performance.

If, for example, we needed some extra money for the family, we might seek part-time work or seek an organisation that offers good pay for part-time work. The basis of our need is for money and convenience. Therefore, motivation stimulation related to these two aspects may be the basis of our performance. The suggestion here is that attachment to the labour market, occupational choice and performance may be related.

Motivation and society: motives that come from the way we live

We have all come across the 'workaholic' who lives only for work, or the person with a vocation who, while not living to work, makes work the driving force of their lives in different ways. These are extreme examples of work values dominating social values. Is there a case for the opposite scenario, where it is the way we live in society that gives us our motivation?

We are not talking here about the transfer of habits; for example, a painstaking craftsman might well be equally fastidious at home, and an accountant might not be able to resist checking the household bills. What is at stake here is whether motivation stems from work or from the way we live.

People have general attitudes to work called orientations to work. There are three broad types:

1. instrumental orientation – work is simply a means to an end;
2. career orientation – where sacrifices are made for future rewards;
3. communal orientation – simply where work and leisure are seamlessly drawn together.

These motivations stem from outside work in the first case, through family-centred life and a desire for material advancement; in the second case, through ambition and the social expectations of getting on; and in the third case,

PEOPLE AT WORK

through a desire to live in a community. These categories are 'ideal types'. The controversial point is that as this big motivation is brought in with the coat in the morning, management can only go along with it. This challenges other motivation theories.

This focus on society as the source of motivation rather than work suggests that society and work may be competing not just for the time of the individual but as the source of motivation. The 'generational' arguments (X,Y,Z) contest that recent historical changes in birth rates together with rapid technological progress has produced cohorts of people with different orientations to life and work. In macro terms, differences between generations can be observed, but explanations for them lack evidence. The studies in this area tend to focus on educated youth rather than the general population. There is a lack of evidence of the intervention of economic upheavals and cultural dynamics in this area.

The location factor

We live in the world, but more precisely we live and work in a specific location. This narrower perspective is more significant to our motivations at work. Suppose a hotel is located in a geographically isolated outpost. Everyone who works there lives in the local village and the hotel is the major employer in the locality. Now, suppose something bad happens at work. For instance, suppose management makes a bad error which causes a grievance in the workforce. In such circumstances, everyone will take the grumble home with them and discuss it with their co-workers out of work. This will have the effect of crystallising and magnifying the grievance. Next morning, they go into work with an anti-management attitude which is thus likely to further sour relations and cause more trouble. However, the example here uses something negative *but the process would work just as well for something positive.*

The principle at stake here is called the integration principle, and it emphasises how such work values can be reinforced or diluted by the degree to which the workforce is integrated in the wider local society. If the workforce is by some means isolated from the wider society, then it is likely that their values of work will be reinforced by life outside work *then brought back to work as an attitude.* The form of isolation may be geographical or related to unsocial hours. The integration argument is that when workers go home and socialise with workers from other industries, 'talking shop' is less likely and grumbles are disarmed by comparisons. In these circumstances, what happens at work stays at work.

The relevance to hospitality is fairly obvious. Employees in the hospitality industry are often physically isolated, live in provided accommodation and work unsocial hours when the rest of the population is at leisure. In these circumstances it would be expected that work values would be fairly dominant values even out of hours, but the message for management is that this reinforcement process can work on both positive and negative raw material.

Motivation and motivating

One of the most common sights in management is to see managers down at heart and blaming themselves when their strategies to motivate their staff appear not to have worked. They attribute the cause to themselves. Yet if there is one message that comes through clearly from the psychologists it is that *motivation is, at best, a game of chance!*

You cannot know another person's needs or how they define themselves. In other words, you don't know what motivates them. You cannot even be sure they have perceived your strategy. If they have and if it works – great. If they haven't or they have and it doesn't – bad luck. The sin in motivation is not getting it wrong but not trying something else. Motivation is a constant process of trial and error. Criticism should fall on those who duck out and not on those who fail.

In a sense, what matters is not so much what motivates but 'what works for me'. The implication here is that as a manager you have to learn from life and experience. We know that some people are better people managers than others, but we also know that people get better at it with experience – that is, providing that they themselves are open to learning. What this means is looking continually at the results of your efforts and being prepared to try different approaches.

This last contention points clearly to one solid fact in the motivation debate – you, the manager, count because as the motivator you will never be neutral in the eyes of those who work for you. In fact, if you ask if there are any certainties, any sure-fire bets in the what motivates stakes, the answer is a qualified yes. We know there are four aspects of work to which an employee is never neutral about. These are:

1. the immediate boss;
2. the pay;
3. their effort;
4. their confidence to do the job.

While you come to see them as satisfiers or, in Herzberg's terms, as dissatisfiers or whether or not they motivate, they are always salient to the amount of drive being applied in the job.

Motivating – where to start?

Sometimes it is easy for managers to overlook obvious sources of motivation. In most occupations the reason why we take the job in the first place influences our self-identity and, therefore, the way we see things in the job. In evaluating aspects of the job, we are, to an extent, justifying our original good sense in taking the job. The message here is that a few clues as to a person's

PEOPLE AT WORK

sense of motivation can be obtained through the selection process. Here the key question is: what does a person bring to a job?

- Graded self-assessment of abilities.
- A preconceived estimate of what and how they can learn.
- A clear view of what they are good at and what they are bad at.
- Task preferences; likes and dislikes.
- Values and value justifications.
- An estimate of what value they bring to the organisation.
- A rationale for why they are there.
- A degree of compatibility between personality and role.

It is not difficult to see that all these self-estimates contain potential uncertainty and inaccuracy. People will overestimate and underestimate their virtues and be vague about reasons. But, it is this uncertainty that provides the building blocks for motivation as the manager and the worker grope their way towards an agreement (psychological contract) as to how the job should be done and how, realistically, it will be done. If you want to de-motivate someone, then make them incompetent! Give them a job they are unsuitable for, don't train them and if you are asking people to learn a new job and don't recognise that initially they will not be fully productive and criticise them, then that is how not to do it.

Notwithstanding the observable fact of individual differences, common sense would suggest that there are a number of actions which may or may not constitute motivation but might register as 'good housekeeping' in this area. These are:

- clear communication – people cannot respond to a stimulus if they cannot see it clearly – the manager must convince that the rewards and the performance are related;
- offering valued rewards;
- not taking too much control;
- recognising achievement – recognition appears in every theoretical scheme, and it accords with our common sense that to recognise achievement will increase performance;
- ensuring that rewards are equitable;
- teaching someone something is an excellent basis for being able to motivate them;
- ensuring that all aspects of employment tell a coherent story.

Further reading

Hekman A. and Lashley, C. (2018) 'Workers in the luxury hospitality industry and motivation – the influence of gender, age and departments', *Research in Hospitality Management*, 7: 115–120.

MOTIVATION **45**

Why read this? It is a very small study based on one hotel and from which you cannot generalise, but it does get inside a luxury hotel and exhibit some differences by age and gender to motivational stimuli. It provides a good entry path into the literature of motivation as it applies to hospitality. In contrast try:

Riley, M., Lockwood, A., Powell-Perry, J. and Baker, M. (1998) 'Job satisfaction, organisation commitment and occupational culture: a case from the UK pub industry', *Progress in Tourism and Hospitality Research*, 4: 1–10.

Why read this? It is a large scale survey in which the method is explicitly described. It has some idiosyncratic findings but not on the principal topic – despite low pay, pub workers like working in pubs. Who knew! All the writers mentioned in this chapter on motivation are listed in the bibliography.

CHAPTER

5 Negative behaviour

Having argued in the last chapter that motivation is not an exact science because we cannot be sure that people will see and respond to our motivational stimuli, we must now try to understand the psychological mechanisms people have to avoid seeing motivational stimuli. Fundamentally, we are looking at what intervenes between the individual's motivational needs and the manager's motivational stimuli that causes the former not to see the latter. This chapter is about awareness and about an acceptance that negative aspects can be present even in positive motivational climates.

Chapter objectives

- to introduce you to the ideas of cognitive dissonance and relative deprivation in understanding negative behaviour;
- to explain the ways of handling negative feelings;
- to show you why these are important in managing people.

We have all, at some time, had the experience of being upset, anxious or angry about something and trying to 'forget it' by immersing ourselves in work. At first it doesn't work; the thoughts that made us anxious keep returning. Sometimes it doesn't work at all. Work and the anxiety compete until the problem goes away or concentration on work eventually triumphs. The point being made here is that we cannot motivate ourselves while we are in any way anxious. If you, as a manager, are trying to motivate a person who is anxious, they simply will not respond, because they will not see what you are doing. The message is that anxiety intervenes in the motivation process. This is why any serious consideration of motivation must include a discussion of the role of, for want of a better phrase, negative aspects.

Our fundamental problem is that we can only deal with the behaviour that presents itself to us. Yet there is a question as to whether there is a direct relationship between the way we feel and the way we behave. Can the former be predicted from the latter? While acknowledging that there must be many times when there is such a direct relationship – for example feeling hungry makes us eat – intuition suggests that may not always be so.

The relationship is unreliable, and it would be wrong to trust it when you are faced only with behaviour. Either with intent, or unconsciously, an individual may distort the way they behave from the genesis of behaviour – feeling.

That uncomfortable feeling of inconsistency

People like to feel that they are intrinsically consistent so that their cognitive states tell a story which they can live with. Whatever their beliefs, attitudes and habits are, they are consistent and compatible. However a moment's reflection would tell us that we do not always behave in a way which represents the way we feel. This is not in itself a problem unless you are a manager faced with trying to understand someone's behaviour. The theory of cognitive dissonance may suggest a helpful framework for understanding the unreliable relationship between feeling and behaviour. (Note: feeling is not the only source of behaviour; instinct and habit are also salient, but we are only concerned here with feeling.)

The theory argues that if we hold inconsistent beliefs, or are forced into actions we do not believe in, or find the reality of life inconsistent with our expectations, we feel psychological discomfort. We cannot walk around forever with such discomfort – it must be 'handled' in some way. The obvious resolution is to take the appropriate action – i.e. change your belief or do something else. We could also put it literally out of mind. But we have two other options; we could blame someone or something else for our predicament or we could rationalise it away. The whole point about blame and rationalisation processes is that they should be automatic – a pre-prepared response. Think of the time you tried to give up something and the kind of excuses you used to yourself when you failed (think of smoking or dieting). The theory does not suggest what we do to render the feeling impotent, only that we must do something. Such as:

1. have a ready-made automatic excuse;
2. blame someone else;
3. put it out of mind (mental reach);
4. take the behavioural route (stop doing it);
5. all of the above.

If only we didn't compare

A pre-requisite of feeling psychological discomfort is to be aware of some adverse conditions. That awareness may result from a comparison and may be dispersed by a different, more favourable comparison. What may intervene between the feeling and the need to rationalise it away, or take action to correct it, will be the location of blame and the degree to which action to alleviate the adverse conditions is actually possible. The more extreme the

PEOPLE AT WORK

feeling of self-blame, the more pressure within to rationalise the condition away or project blame onto someone else – e.g. management, the unions, human nature! Indeed, projection of blame may be a form of rationalisation. Furthermore, if you can't see that 'action is possible', then the pressure to rationalise is that much greater. This is not a psychological fancy; it is the daily reality in hospitality, where there is a clear economic disparity between the guest and the service worker. Staff who are living at a subsistence level go to work in a hotel and find themselves in close proximity to rich tourists. This requires some kind of psychological adjustment or adaption on the part of the employees if conflict is to be avoided. The theory of relative deprivation argues that feelings of psychological discomfort can be regulated by the comparisons we make. We can make ourselves really unhappy by making invidious comparisons. We can also modify our negative feeling by choosing a less invidious comparison.

In considering how a person responds to a feeling of psychological discomfort, two adaption processes are important: distortion and dilution. The greatest pressure for us to distort comes from negative feelings. This makes the handling of grievances one of the most difficult aspects of people management. One possible outcome of this process is the substitution of one grievance for another. Frustrated promotion may come out as a demand for more money. Difficulty with a supervisor may come out as a grumble about the amount of work. Always assuming grievance is voiced at all, the result might be simply leaving employment. This process of rationalisation though substitution is encouraged by authority, which is always slightly intimidating. There is always a danger that subordinates will not say what they really mean or want to say. Similarly, it is all too easy to overlook the fact that some people may not have the vocabulary to express what they feel. However, by far the most common influence on a grievance is the individual's perception of the likely outcome. Will it be successful and what will it cost? All this adds doubt and makes the actual interpretation that much more difficult. Notwithstanding the problem of distortion, there is yet a further complication – that of dilution.

Any job contains a number of attributes, and it must be obvious that each of these attributes will attract a different intensity of feeling. Therefore a feeling of dissatisfaction over one attribute may be ameliorated by satisfaction with another. For example, a chef may hate the management, hate the pay or be indifferent to the work group but love what he or she actually does. A poor pay rise may produce a mild grumble, but a sudden de-skilling would produce an explosion! In other words, satisfaction and dissatisfaction trade with each other. This is why a small thing can so often trigger a surprisingly hostile reaction.

Conceptual framework

Figure 5.1 attempts to conceptualise the passage of a feeling of psychological discomfort going through the influence of dilution of intensity through an assessment of possible outcome to the individual handling the feeling.

NEGATIVE BEHAVIOUR

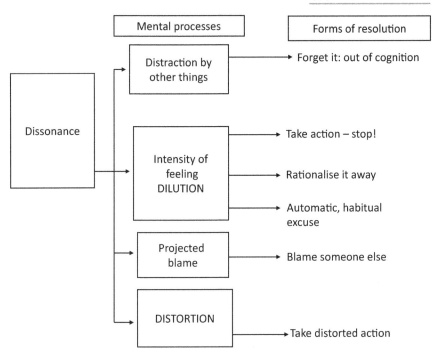

Figure 5.1 Dissonance and its resolution

It is clear now that the link between dissatisfaction and behaviour may not be direct; a lot of things can get in the way. Individuals may endure abject deprivation, they may rationalise their grievance away, and their resultant behaviour may be more strategic than relevant to their feelings. All this adds doubt. Certainly it would be difficult to predict that a particular form of behaviour would follow from a specific grievance, even if it could be identified! This problem of identifying cause is unfortunately not a simple one of seeking to unravel the processes of rationalisation and strategy; there is the serious problem of multiple causation and cumulative causation. There may be many things wrong at the same time and, while they may not all be pressing, accumulation can occur with the result that the behaviour may be only looking to the most salient of the grievances, making life difficult for possible solutions. It is not just a case of 'the pay's rotten, the tools are falling apart and I can't stand the supervisor'. Any one issue can cause a variety of dissatisfactions.

How should we approach grievances?

It is not management's task to solve all the personal problems of the staff, therefore the first question posed is: how far should managers get involved? One obvious answer is to the extent that productivity is being adversely

PEOPLE AT WORK

affected by the grievance. That is not so easy to judge, and it may be acting too late. If they are out of the door, there is no point in intervening. Anyway, this whole area is a bit of a minefield. One man's solution may be another man's grievance – you may unknowingly rob Peter to pay Paul. In terms of decision-making we are in the realm of every form of uncertainty. Is there a way through? Well, there are three considerations here – philosophy, authority and procedure.

An appropriate philosophy?

If you went to the doctor complaining of a pain in your shoulder, he or she would examine you and possibly locate the cause of your problem as something wrong with your forearm. He or she would, therefore, treat the forearm. In other words, look at the symptoms, find the cause and treat the cause. All very logical, scientific and sensible. Yet in the case of management, wrong! Here is a point where management and science part company. Managers must treat the symptoms as well as the causes. If someone says they have a problem with pay but you have found the cause to be the relations with the supervisor, both the 'real' problem and the worker's own interpretation have to be treated seriously because they are both real to the individual.

Your authority

Your authority is a barrier. Perhaps the sensible way forward here is to conduct your authority in such a way as to be seen as 'being approachable'. One way of solving this is a willingness to come out of 'your territory'. We are not like animals, but we are possessive about bits of space. Listening in another person's space at least helps to break down the barrier of your authority.

Procedure

The importance of having a recognised procedure for grievances is that it introduces an element of justice into the affair and at the same time sidesteps the problems of authority and inarticulateness. It also has the merit of taking some of the emotion out of the grievance. By going through the procedure, the person has taken some action to alleviate the psychological discomfort. What is left is not the desire for a full settlement of their case but the desire for justice. The procedure at least offers an outcome, if not the desired outcome. There are a lot of problems associated with grievance procedures, but when they work they are an attribute to labour management and can prevent people settling their grievances with their feet – i.e. walking out.

Good habits

- Avoid promises.
- Take what people say seriously.
- Investigate thoroughly.
- Avoid favours.
- Avoid reciprocal 'deals'.

CHAPTER

6 Commitment, job satisfaction and empowerment

In this chapter we build on our knowledge of motivation and particularly on that important aspect of motivation we call job satisfaction. Two questions need to be addressed here; how are the intrinsic needs of an individual met by their work? And, in the context of hospitality, where labour mobility if known to be high, how is job satisfaction related to commitment? Are we committed to an organisation because our job is satisfying, or do we find the job satisfying because we are committed to it? The importance of commitment to the hospitality industry is that a stable workforce is more likely to offer quality service than one which is constantly churning over.

Chapter objectives

- to show that job satisfaction is constructed out of trade-offs;
- to show the relationship between satisfaction and commitment;
- to show the relationship between organisational change and empowerment.

The hospitality context

If you are a regular customer at an establishment, you want to see familiar faces and staff who recognise you. It is an ideal state and speaks of employee commitment as something to be fostered. You get quality from commitment and job satisfaction; therefore, managers strive to keep good staff.Economics, however, has a different take and demands a numerically flexible workforce to cope with fluctuating demand (see Chapter 11). There is a built-in attrition between quality and profitability that crystallises the issue of employee commitment. This is the context in which people are managed in hospitality.

A concern for quality needs employee commitment

The moment an organisation adopts a policy which emphasises quality, then it has to rethink its approach to motivation. In a service industry where customers are dealt with face-to-face, there can be no question of high quality co-existing with high levels of labour turnover. Even when there is an efficient training function, the constant appearance of new faces prevents a degree of continuity taking root. Such continuity is essential to good quality service.

It is a concern for quality that has refocused the perspective from 'the problems and benefits of high labour turnover' (we explore some of the benefits in later chapters) towards the idea of employee commitment. In other words, emphasis is now on how we can keep our valued employees. Keeping them automatically implies the question of how we can motivate them to a level of performance beyond what might be expected from secure employment to a level based on taking responsibility and being actively involved. To have this greater expectation of employees is essential because continuity alone does not make for quality service. There is always the chance that the performance of a stable workforce can go stale.

Commitment by employees automatically means greater commitment from managers, who must possess a wider range of motivational techniques than was the case with a workforce that was ever-changing. It is true that in most service organisations there are always stable and unstable elements in the workforce. However, it is clear from the analysis of the labour markets of labour intensive service industries that managers have, in the past, chosen to manage the whole workforce in a style appropriate to an unstable element of that workforce. This changes once quality becomes a priority. Management policies must then have a style and content that suits the needs of a stable workforce.

Whilst it is easy to imagine the relationship between job satisfaction and labour turnover, the relationship between job satisfaction and commitment is more complex and is, in some respects, rather surprising. One would expect labour turnover to decline as job satisfaction and commitment increase. However, what is the direction of influence between job satisfaction and commitment? If an employee is more satisfied, are they also more committed or does commitment cause satisfaction?

To understand the relationship between this trio of concepts it is necessary to start with one behavioural aspect – that of people leaving. Whether they leave or stay does act as an indicator of both job satisfaction and commitment. However, the key to this matter is the pivotal concept of job satisfaction. It is pivotal because it will be shown that both labour turnover and commitment are dependent upon it. If a new perspective is taken on job satisfaction, one which is not concerned with questions of what motivates, then the role of job satisfaction becomes clearer. The new perspective is to see it as a process and not just as content which gratifies needs.

Why do people stay with an organisation?

- Habit? – a comfortable feeling like an old overcoat.
- The self-justifying nature of routine?
- You come to believe in what you do, no matter what you thought at first?
- A need for social identity?
- A reciprocal exchange with an organisation? (The psychological contract.)
- A calculative-instrumental exchange? (The psychological contract.)
- Fear of change and new horizons?
- A need for purposeful life activity?

These reasons are not mutually exclusive, and often their boundaries are blurred. Nor are people always aware of the reasons for staying. Almost by definition the rationale becomes a habit.

Every individual makes their own job satisfaction; it is a process

Motivation theory shows us what elements of employment and work can motivate. In motivational theory, individual differences between people and changes within the same person in different circumstances and over time are explained by different levels of individual need and changes to those needs. What has to be explained is how changes come about. In other words, accepting changes in personal need, how does the individual construe these changes? There must a process at work here involving both personal needs and situational variables. Note what is being said here, that job satisfaction is not just a matter of satisfying needs but also of making the social and physical environment work for them.

Every individual makes their own satisfaction. The individual puts together their psychological and social needs with all the elements of the situation as they find it and produces a concept of job satisfaction of their own. In other words, job satisfaction is manufactured – very much a bespoke creation. The assumption is that even if individuals are not rational or realistic the situation imposes both on them. Whatever satisfaction there is to be had must lie in their objective situation. In other words, it is only their situation which can satisfy their actual needs. (From the previous chapter this brings together the needs theorists with Snyder and Williams.)

It cannot come from anywhere else. Even ambitions and dreams have their centre of gravity in the person's current situation. The expression 'where do I go from here' captures this notion of things being rooted in the reality of the present. This is not to say that everybody will be able to create an acceptable level of job satisfaction. For some, the level of satisfaction created remains unsatisfactory, which may in turn lead to labour turnover.

There are five processes that enable people to create their own satisfaction. Each of them works through either changes of needs or are responses to stimuli from the work environment. The processes are:

1. information processing;
2. selecting particular attributes;

COMMITMENT, JOB SATISFACTION AND EMPOWERMENT

3. ordering attributes;
4. trade-offs;
5. reselection and reordering over time.

For the purposes of understanding these processes it would be useful to work from a hypothetical example. An individual has some personal needs which relate to work. These needs are expressed in a range of job attributes which they look for in selecting a job and hope to find in the job. Not all attributes of a job are selected, and those that are exist in a rank order of some kind; for example, working in a stimulating group comes before pay, which ranks above interesting tasks, etc. All very well, but how does it actually work? As the sole source of satisfaction is the working environment, the individual takes in the information there and reassesses their range and rank of favoured job attributes. It is no good wanting autonomy if the place runs on close supervision!

What then happens when some of the favoured job attributes are not available in that particular environment? One solution is to leave but another is to 'trade-off' the costs and benefits in order to get a 'working set of job attribute satisfiers'. For example, the pay is poor but the boss is nice; the group is attractive even if the work is boring etc. In this way job satisfaction is manufactured by the individual. This does not mean that the person becomes deliriously happy, but it does mean that there is enough in the job to make them feel comfortable in coming to work. It must be said that if there are particular and intensely felt needs that are not available, then the most likely form of behaviour is to leave.

What is commitment? Is it just motivation by another name?

No. It is a conscious affirmation of loyalty to something or somebody. As commitment 'in secret' is rather a redundant idea, the concept implies some form of behaviour which openly expresses this state of loyalty. It may be as mundane as not leaving or something more affirmative such as extra motivation. A further complication comes with the focus of commitment. Within the work environment there are many potential targets: what are you committing to?

- Job commitment.
- Tasks within a job.
- Occupational commitment.
- Career commitment.
- Organisational commitment.
- Work group attachment.
- Commitment to a profession.

It would be easy to fall into the trap of thinking that because the organisation is the actual situation for all these types of commitment they are all variations

56 PEOPLE AT WORK

on the theme of organisational commitment. They are not. If the primary aim is to create organisational commitment, then loyalty to a task, an occupation, a profession or to personal advancement can run counter to the concept of the organisation as the emotional home and source of stimulus.

What is organisational commitment?

Definitions abound, but perhaps the clearest way to describe organisational commitment is to draw a picture of the behaviour that is likely to be found in an employee who is specifically committed to an organisation.

Beyond the obvious likelihood of punctuality, reliability and cooperativeness, three deeper aspects of commitment may be present and visible. These are:

1. an emotional attachment to the aims and values of the organisation. This attachment is often expressed through pride in the name of the company;
2. a willingness that goes beyond normative expectations;
3. being prepared to push instrumentality into the background. Notice, pushing it away from performance but not abandoning it!

In a sense, commitment has one advantage for management over motivation in that whilst motivation has to be demonstrated to be acknowledged, commitment actually has to be openly declared in some way by both parties. Commitment implies going public. A common theme that runs through the ideas on commitment is the concept of exchange – that is, giving energy and time in return for rewards.

This brings together the basic ideas of motivation theory with ideas on work environment in that people come to organisations with needs, desires and skills. If the organisation provides the opportunity for abilities to be utilised and for some needs to be satisfied in a consistent and dependable way, then the possibility of commitment is enhanced. By contrast, when this is not the case, then the chance of achieving commitment is diminished.

This idea of exchange not only reconfirms that the instrumental nature of employment is never far from the surface but also that it fits exactly into one of the key elements of the job satisfaction process – that of exchanging attributes. Here we have stumbled upon the link between job satisfaction and commitment.

The exchange idea must, in operation, be a judgement made after some time; e.g. 'Let's take a rain check,' 'I'm giving this much and I'm getting this back,' 'yes, it's worth committing,' 'no, it is not worth it'. The process of forming a judgement by summing up both sides of an equation is only possible through the job satisfaction process itself. In other words, only after manipulating and altering valued attributes through an exchange process and then seeing if satisfaction is attainable is a decision to commit made. If this is true, then we would expect to see commitment following job satisfaction with perhaps a small time lag. This is indeed the case, but there is an extra twist in the tale.

COMMITMENT, JOB SATISFACTION AND EMPOWERMENT   57

If the progress of an employee is examined over a period of time, starting from the moment they agree to join the organisation, then a pattern emerges that slightly changes the relationship between job satisfaction and commitment just described. At this point two new terms are introduced. These are: entrenchment and re-commitment.

A brief overview of the progress of a newcomer into an organisation would be through a series of stages.

Stage	Behaviour
Pre-entry stage	Anticipation
Early stage	Initiation through socialisation
Settling in	Time to evaluate job satisfaction
Settled in	If job satisfaction is high, then the employee re-commits. If job satisfaction is low, then the employee does not recommit.

What is happening here is that commitment is dependent not just on job satisfaction but on job satisfaction being maintained to the time when a reappraisal or 'taking a rain check' takes place. In other words, achieving job satisfaction at the very beginning is good but not a precursor of commitment. If, and only if, job satisfaction is maintained does the employee commit. What follows this commitment is a form of entrenchment whereby the employee, so to speak, puts down roots.

What is the psychological value of commitment?

The real value of organisational commitment is in its capacity to facilitate change. If the individual is focused on the organisation rather than the job or the career or profession, then the reception accorded to change is slightly different than if commitment was not present.

In the chapter on motivation it was suggested there is a need to expand the concept a little. When applying an incentive, what are we trying to achieve?

- To get people to work harder?
- Be more loyal?
- Be flexible?
- Be prepared to abandon old skills?
- Be prepared to learn new skills?

The last three objectives all carry the fear of change and require cooperation. The committed environment has an advantage over mere 'good motivational practices' in this important area.

The lessons for managers

The main point for hospitality managers is that given that they want a stable workforce then job satisfaction must be a goal. However, the strategy must be to encourage satisfaction at the outset through a good induction process but more importantly have an early appraisal at between four to six months to see if satisfaction has been maintained. The actual point when the employee considers commitment and entrenchment cannot be known, but it is almost certainly to be within the first six months.

If commitment is a desired aim, then it can be reinforced by policies which make the employee a stakeholder in the organisation. Profit sharing and shareholding schemes work well in the context of commitment. In a sense, they are the 'public' commitment of management to the committed employee.

If the trend towards organisation commitment is seen as a means to create a new organisational context, then the 'active' principle within that context is the concept of *empowerment*. In fact, the ideas of commitment and empowerment work in tandem and form the basis of the concept of 'quality'. In order to understand what empowerment is, it is necessary to recognise that it is about organisational behaviour and about change. It is a new form of organisational behaviour and structure which has come about because of a perceived need for organisational responsiveness and which is itself the mechanism that enables organisations to be responsive.

The idea of empowerment is perhaps often misunderstood. Such misunderstanding has led to cynicism about the 'authenticity' of empowerment schemes. Responsibility without power is one cynical view. In a sense, this scepticism is justified because to work properly empowerment has to be done well. This requires management to realise what an enormous change is required of the incumbent of an empowered role. For empowerment to work properly, both managers and workers have to understand the real implications of what the change actually means.

What is empowerment?

Empowerment is incorporating into an employee's role the authority and means to be responsive to customer requirements. It enables the employees to be responsive by ensuring that the necessary rules of order within the organisation do not interfere with the performance of a task which the customer requires.

Put simply, this means that empowerment is giving the employees the right to 'break the rules' to serve the customer. In a real sense this is a risky strategy for management because 'rules' are always necessary to an organisation. It is a balance between organisational rules and discretion which must be available quickly.

The idea that employees should have authority and take responsibility for their actions is not new, but it has never before been allied to a business objective of ensuring customers receive a defined quality of product or service. What is new about the empowerment movement is that it takes a basic idea from motivation theory – that is, that employees respond to autonomy and achievement – and places it in an overall design of the production or service. Here human performance is built-in to the product or service itself rather than being just a factor of production like working capital.

The logic of organisational change

Perhaps the best way to see the differences in philosophies between straight-forward good management of workers and the empowerment idea is to see how the empowerment movement came about. The logic of giving employees authority stems directly from three factors which have come together simultaneously.

1. The advances in computer and telecommunication systems have led to an increased ability to communicate and an increased ability to specify and control the content of people's jobs.
2. Technology has granted the ability to specify and therefore to standardise a product or service. At the same time market competition has led to the need to use that ability to specify and standardise to create product differentiation through added value.
3. A desire to get closer to the customer. The idea that companies must understand the need of their customers has led to the simple conclusion that means getting close to them.

These three 'big' ideas have led to a number of organisational changes.

1. The height of the organisational pyramid is being lowered. Organisations are getting flatter with fewer and fewer levels of authority between the strategy decision-makers and the shop floor.
2. If being able to respond to customer needs is the aim, then flexible work practices are essential. The implication here is that roles need to be defined broadly and must 'not be set in stone'.
3. If understanding the customers' needs is the aim, then those people who deal directly with the customers are important employees. The new emphasis is to focus on the performance of those employees who deal directly with customers.
4. To take advantage of the flatter organisation, the flexible work practices and the feedback from customers there has to be an organisational culture that values change.

In a sense, these organisational changes are 'the context' of empowerment rather than leading directly to it. What the organisational changes imply is good human relations management with a focus on development and on

PEOPLE AT WORK

individuals. What leads directly to the notion of empowerment is the realisation that it is *never easy for an organisation to be responsive* and that there is *no one ideal structure that will guarantee such responsiveness*. Organisation theory has in the past suggested two polar types of organisation: the bureaucratic structure and the organic structure. Whilst the former is 'rule bound' the latter is more open, less rule bound and capable of rapid change. Obviously the organic model is more responsive than the bureaucratic one. However, the question that remains in the case of hospitality is if it is responsive enough.

The modern answer to this question is no! Organisational structures need rules, need goals of order, otherwise nothing can be achieved. By definition, this places a limit on how rapidly a structure can change itself. It is this reasoning that has led to the conclusion that people can be more responsive than structures and that therefore to 'go that extra mile' for the customer requires a personal response rather than an organisation response. This is the heart of empowerment. This is the logic that leads to the idea of giving people the ability to override organisational rules and norms to meet specific customer needs.

The limits of empowerment

It must be clear from the context that empowerment is not about management giving up their responsibility and giving away their authority to employees who can do what they like. This is a recipe for chaos. What empowerment is about is giving employees authority and decision-making power within parameters defined by two variables:

1. the definition and nature of the actual product and service being offered;
2. the boundaries of customer perception of that product or service and the probable range of discrepancy between the organisation's definition of the product and service and the customer's definition.

In other words, the employee cannot change the product or service, but they can intervene between the organisation's idea of what the product or service is and the customer's perception of it. Where they disagree is where the responsiveness of empowerment plays its major role.

Differences in expectations, the requirement for minor changes and for minor additions, the idiosyncratic nature of feedback on satisfaction – all these aspects are best handled by a person rather than by a set of rules and roles.

The real limits on empowerment come in two forms:

1. control over resources;
2. the scope of the product and service itself.

Phony empowerment is when the employee only has the 'power' to make a profuse 'apology' but cannot put the problem right. There must be sufficient resources under the control of the person to be able to put things right. The danger here is that they may promise more than can be delivered or that they may extend the product or service beyond that laid down (and costed) by management. The resource problem in the context of empowerment requires a closer relationship between managers and workers.

The management–worker relationship in the context of empowerment

Clearly there is a strong element of trust required by the idea of empowerment. This is why the concept is so closely linked to the policy of encouraging organisational commitment from employees. Commitment and trust come out of the same knapsack. Where there is a blurring of boundaries and rules, and where there is a high level of subjectivity, trust becomes the significant element in the manager–worker response to the customer.

However, trust is not all that is required; knowledge of the product/service and knowledge of the organisation form the background to trust.

If an employee is going to respond to a customer they must know:

- what the product or service is! This means knowing its limits and its position in relation to other products or services;
- what the organisation can and cannot do! False promises end in tears. There are limits in terms of production and in terms of costs;
- the rules and norms of the organisation. To be sensitive to the areas of discretion.

This knowledge cannot come about by accident. It requires careful role definition and training.

Change and learning

It was suggested earlier that the logic of empowerment is based on the idea that organisations, even organic organisations, cannot be quickly responsive to customers. There are limits to how adaptive an organisation can be. This is also true of individual managers. They cannot do everything, know everything. It follows, therefore, that encouraging learning by employees takes away from managers the potential burden of knowledge overload. Even if they have the knowledge, managers cannot remember or be aware of everything at the moment it becomes required by a customer.

In terms of technical production, the normal situation would be managers laying down the product and system and faults being picked up as they occur. This is a 'deficiency-based' approach to quality. The problem is that it is 'backwards facing'. When a problem occurs it is handled. The empowerment approach is the key to prevent problems, to be proactive in terms of quality. The approach required here is one of continuous learning by the employee.

PEOPLE AT WORK

The development of this learning begins with training employees to reflect on the quality of their own work. This is followed by giving them the authority to change their own work methods to improve the product. The final stage is to incorporate the capacity to reflect and change into the definition of the product or service itself.

Further reading

Ogaard, T., Marnburg, E. and Larsen, S. (2008) 'Perceptions of organizational structure in the hospitality industry: consequences for commitment, job satisfaction and perceived performance', *Tourism Management*, 29, 4: 661–671.

Why read this? This is interesting because they use perceptions of the organisation as the determinant of satisfaction and commitment. The old organic-mechanistic contrasting frames of reference work here.

Shapira, Z. (1981) 'Making trade-offs between job attributes', *Organizational Behaviour and Human Performance*, 28, 3: 331–355.

Why read this? In this chapter we discussed the way individuals curate their own job satisfaction. Here is a rare piece of research that shows how the process of trade-offs between attributes of a job actual works.

Riley, M. (1996) 'Interpersonal communication: the contribution of dyadic analysis to the understanding of tourism behaviour', *Progress in Tourism and Hospitality Research*, 1, 2: 115–124.

Why read this? This paper is about service encounters and how satisfaction can be derived from a job made up of continually dealing with people.

CHAPTER

7 Group behaviour and teams

You will become aware that dealing with a group of individuals is not quite the same as dealing with one individual. The approach, the skills – something more is required when you have to manage a group of people. Managers like to talk of teams and teamwork, but these words are difficult to define, let alone achieve. Giving a set of individuals a group task to do won't, of itself, form them into groups. Putting on a coloured shirt and running on to a field with others similarly attired won't make them a team! Yet teamwork can be seen and felt – it is a tangible thing. The real problem is that we organise people into groups, call them teams, but don't look to see if they are actually behaving like groups or teams. The words 'group' and 'team' tend to be used conterminously, but one expression is central to both concepts and that is 'common identity'.

Chapter objectives

- to introduce perspectives on what it means to work together;
- to introduce 'group process';
- to introduce the notion of group identity;
- to differentiate the management task of managing groups from that of individuals.

The hospitality context

Here is the great motivational dilemma for management in hospitality; tasks are both individualistic and group simultaneously. A waiter/waitress brings a meal to a table – it is an individual task. However, not only is that meal produced by others in a process and the restaurant equipment used by the server shared by other servers, but the very appeal of the restaurant is dependent on the quality of service throughout. The ambiance of the room is not just a function of décor but of the relationships between servers and servers and their customers – this is group task. Hospitality tasks are individual and group at the same time, and, in a sense, all the issues surrounding the distribution of tips crystallise this conundrum.

PEOPLE AT WORK

The question is should managers motivate individuals or address them as a groups, or both. In Chapter 9 we see the importance of identity, with its connotations of group attachment.Furthermore, in action, group process tells us that group attachment is both vital and automatic – groups are always the context of individual tasks in hospitality. This why hospitality is so concerned to set an organisational culture that reflects actual hospitality and does this through normative control – that is, management demonstrating through leadership what ought to happen.

In Chapter 4 we learnt about the location factor. Hospitality workers are often isolated from the general public and drawn together by unsocial hours and physical location. This encourages group formation, which has to be considered by managers because it will be brought into work.

Group formation

Go into a restaurant or kitchen or to any behind the scenes area and you will often see some physical similarities between people working in the same area. They might, for example, be roughly the same age or the same sex or both. They might all have little education or all be graduates or all have the same social origin. What you will notice is that as the similarities pile up – the more homogeneous the people become – the more you tend to think of them as a group and the more they may see themselves as having a common identity. It is not that physical similarity causes groups to form; it is just that they may kick the thought process in that direction. With some confidence we can say that the more homogeneous the group the more likely it is to see itself as a group; in other words, have a group identity. This possibility of a set of individuals having a group identity is important to the management of people and particularly to the organisation of teams.

It is very easy to fall into the trap of thinking that managing people is an activity involving problems between them (the workers) and us (the management). A few minutes' acquaintance with people management will introduce you to another significant dimension – the relationships between individual workers and between groups of workers. This relationship, if you like, between 'them' and 'them' is just as crucial to the technological process and productivity achievement as the relationship between management and workers.

Management's interest in understanding group behaviour is founded on four premises.

1. If people behave differently when they are part of a group than when they are just a set of individuals, it is essential for managers to be able to recognise when a set of individuals is a group;
2. Because productivity is achieved in different ways by a group as by individuals, it is essential to be able to recognise the features that produce productivity in groups;

GROUP BEHAVIOUR AND TEAMS   65

3. Although managers have the choice of organising work either on a group basis or an individual basis (subject to technological constraints), in real life the distinction is not always so clear. Often work is organised either in an individualistic mode with group overtones or the other way around. Being able to assess the productivity implications of this is an important managerial skill;

4. When is a group a team? If it is either, does it need leadership? If so, are there any special reasons that make the role of the leader more crucial in some circumstances than others? This is a difficult area – leadership and teamwork. What is clear, however, is that managers should at least appreciate their role as leaders and be able to see when the label 'team' might be appropriate.

The two central questions raised here are: when is a set of individuals a group? And, on what does group productivity depend? There are two clues to the first question – if they behave like a group and if they display own-group favouritism. At this stage, this is not too helpful, but the idea of favouring your own group has obvious implications for intergroup relations. In the case of productivity, if managers are going to organise work on a group basis, which is as a set of interdependent tasks, then there must be something in it for management, which is higher output. If a set of individuals working alone could produce the same or greater output, why organise it on a group basis? The implication here is that groups have some special quality that individuals lack – what is it? To understand both these questions the place to start is what psychology calls 'group process'.

Group process

There are four principal components of this process: conformity to 'norms'; cohesiveness in performance; successful image; and attachment. It is described as a process because each component is dependent upon the other three. To understand this relationship it is probably best to begin with what we can actually observe – conformity to norms and cohesion. Not only is it observable, but we can feel it ourselves. We are all individuals, we proclaim thus, yet on occasions we dress and behave in the particular way which is expected of us. As long as everybody else does it, it remains a social convention, a group norm. Put on a coloured jersey and run onto a field and we are part of something which is more than just ourselves. Jogging is less boring and less tiring when done with others.

As they are central to the process – what are group norms? They are ideas in the minds of members of what members should do, ought to do and are expected to do in prescribed circumstances. The character of a norm is both that of policeman, in the sense that if we behave in a way that departs from the norm the group will, in some way, punish us back into line, and a secret policeman, in that we may prevent ourselves from departing from the norm by feeling guilty. If this is what group norms are, how do they form? It is essentially a social process. Obviously at the very beginning there are no norms, so a simultaneous process of interaction begins in which each member emits

PEOPLE AT WORK

a certain behaviour (talking, exhibiting an attitude, expressing an opinion, posture, dress, manner, speech, etc.) which is either accepted or rejected by others. After a while, each member is aware of how far they can go and what is acceptable and unacceptable. There will, of course, be individual differences and varying interaction patterns. In a sense, this is the 'mechanics' of norm formation; it doesn't really explain the norms that result. In those stakes there are a number of contenders, notably the majority view, consistency, leadership and consensus.

In practice, groups tend to have a wide range of norms, even sometimes covering behaviour away from the group. There are a number of certainties here. You can be sure that there will be norms of performance in relation to quantity and quality, what we think of the management, particular managers, the food, the pay, punctuality and other groups. Norms are one of the defining qualities of groups, but they don't actually produce the productivity; what does that is cohesion.

If normative behaviour is 'expected' behaviour, then cohesive behaviour is 'anticipated' behaviour. The productivity of a group depends on its cohesiveness; the ability of its members to work 'like a machine' anticipating each other's behaviour. Without the benefits of cohesion you might as well break it up into a set of individual tasks (assuming that is a possibility).

Normative behaviour and cohesiveness are two tangible outcomes of group formation, but there is another such outcome. Over time, a group will create for itself a self-image and a reputational image in the outside environment. What seems clear is that this image must be one of success – defined in its own terms. The point here is that the group's way of defining success should be management's way as well. This is not automatic, and it is possible for groups to define themselves in an anti-management mode.

So far, it has been suggested that groups have norms, can achieve cohesion and define themselves as successful, but all this depends on members wanting to be part of the group. The glue which binds them is the degree of attachment of each member. Break the attachment and the rest falls apart.

What we have explored here is a *circular* process or dynamic, which is captured in figure 7.1.

To be productive, the group must be cohesive and to be that it must be successful in achieving its norms, all of which depends on the maintenance of attachment.

A number of consequences appear to be relevant to managers.

- Managers must not expect an individual to give their best personal performance level in a group task (unless it coincides with the group norm).
- Productivity depends on cohesion in a group task.
- To break a group norm is to break cohesion and put productivity at risk.

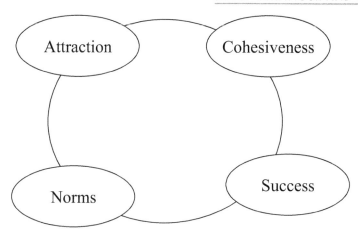

Figure 7.1 Group process

Group process is not an abstraction or just a theory – it can be seen. What you see from the outside is the degree of cohesion. Just a few minutes watching a kitchen brigade can tell you if they are anticipating each other. If that anticipation is not there, then simply calling them a group won't make them anything more than a set of individuals who happen to be all wearing white.

Group identity

To understand group identity we must start from self-identity. Self-identity is how you describe yourself to yourself – not in terms of personality traits, but in terms of how you place yourself in terms of your world view. By contrast, we make up our social identity from the groups we affiliate with. In other words, our social identity draws us towards our group identities. We do not have to be physical members of a group to identify with a group.

At the heart of group process is the idea of attachment. If groups are about conformity why do we do it? Why attach ourselves to a group? Membership is rarely compulsory even at work. In fact, one of the ways by which we might be able to tell, from the outside, if a set of people is a group is whether they display group favouritism.

Part of our self-identity comes from affiliations to groups. These attachments may be simply emotion association or real membership but they become defining qualities – what we are. As group affiliations are part of our identity, we will invest our *commitment with a positive character*. In other words, we seek something positive through group associations. Crucially, this means that we will favour any group to which we are affiliated. The behavioural

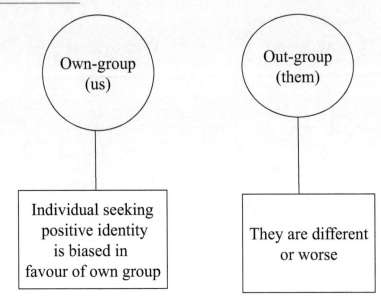

Figure 7.2 Own-group and out-group

effect of this is called own-group bias. As we would favour our own-group, we would define it as different and better than some other identified group – the out-group. Figure 7.2 illustrates this concept.

The importance of this idea is that first of all it puts onto any group a characteristic that can be seen from the outside, which is favouritism of the own-group, which can thus be used as an identifying characteristic. Second, the concept of own-groups and out-groups suggests a framework for understanding intergroup behaviour.

What is being said here is that attachment carries a positive quality, which means that one way of identifying a set of individuals as a real group is if they are clearly favouring themselves and have a clear out-group which they deprecate. Here is a basis for understanding relationships between groups.

Intergroup relations

If we have two groups who are in some way in competition with each other, then we might expect them to see each other in terms of own-groups and out-groups and find ways of defining themselves as better than the others. However, the case of competition is only the obvious one. What is being suggested here is that groups must have some other set of people who they distinguished themselves from: 'they are not us and we are not them, thank goodness!' This form of intergroup relation can be kept on purely a perceptual level, in which case it is of only mild interest to managers. Alas, it rarely stays at this harmless level and can intrude into operational matters as lack of cooperation and have serious implications for status and prestige, not to mention pay comparisons. Front office and housekeeping, kitchen and restaurant all have built-in conflicts, but they are all supposed to be on the same side! If each saw the other as an out-group, then operational problems could ensue.

The organisation of work – individualistic or group

The real problem with understanding groups is that work itself rarely falls simply into either a group mode of operation or an individual mode. Most work processes have overtones of both. It would be appropriate at this point to differentiate purely individual work from purely group work.

Individual work:

- totally autonomous tasks;
- independently resourced;
- only vertical communication required;
- individual differences in status only accepted.

Group work:

- an interdependent set of tasks;
- uniform standards required;
- shared resources;
- competition for scarce resources.

A kitchen would clearly fall towards the group category, with independent tasks brought together by interdependence of timing and standard. A restaurant is essentially a set of individual tasks which are surrounded by group overtones, namely the need for uniformity of standards and the distribution of equipment and customers. Below are useful ways of seeing work groups.

- *The technical group.* To what degree or in what combination is the work organised on a group or individual basis?
- *The social group.* A social group may form even when the tasks are individualistic. For example, a group of waiters who are the same age and nationality may form a group which will bring group process to bear on what is essentially individual work.
- *The earnings group.* Fundamentally, the pay system should follow the technical system. If the task is a genuine group task, why not use a group

PEOPLE AT WORK

incentive scheme? Ideas such as pooled tips are an acknowledgement that in a restaurant individual tasks and effort exist in a group setting.

The important point here is that these formations should not conflict with each other. You cannot do much about social group formation, but certainly the pay system and the work system should be in harmony.

Leadership and groups

It is quite easy to spot sets of individuals who are not yet a group. They meet and someone says 'what shall we do now?' or 'who is going to start first?' or 'who is going to do what?' Eventually someone makes a decision. At work this isn't usually left to simply emerge; it is given to the appointed leader to make. Herein lies a problem. If the leader is appointed, are they part of the group, sharing its group process? A common sentiment such as 'you can't be "one of us" and expect them to respect you' suggests that the leader is outside the group. What this expression really means is that groups have norms of both a work-orientated and social character and that they are interwoven and tend to be pervasive outside work as well. The basic argument is that too much social closeness undermines authority. The contrary argument would be that the 'distance' between the leader and the led would itself be a group norm. This argument suggests that leaders can be within groups. To see the real problem, it is best to look first at the case of the emergent leader; through a rather comical example.

The scene is a boatload of shipwrecked souls, cast out on the ocean with not a sailor aboard. They need a leader. Let us suppose one of their number stands up and shouts 'Follow me; I shall lead you to safety'. They might well push him or her overboard, but a challenge has been issued. If everyone in the boat, however conditionally, acquiesces to that person's leadership, they have all simultaneously agreed to be inferior to the leader. This is the group's first norm! Thus, the emergence of a leader and the embryo formation of a group occur causally and simultaneously. This gives the emergent leader a running start (if they are no good they can still push him or her overboard!).

In the world of work, however, most leaders are appointed. This gives them the disadvantage of not knowing the group norms but the advantage of having a ready-made 'distance' from the lead. Sometimes leaders are appointed from the group. They have the advantage of knowing the group's norms but the disadvantage of having to make more 'distance' and reconcile conflicting interests and loyalties. This is not an arid academic debate, because the question of whether or not the leader is part of the group becomes particularly crucial when, as in the hospitality industry, quality standards are subjective and require some form of normative agreement as to what is good, proper or expected. No leader can be everywhere checking on everything, and if the standards are subjectively measured, then group consensus as to what is good turned into a norm is the maintenance process. This does not excuse the leader from example and vigilance but does embroil them in the group process that sets and maintains the standards.

The role of any leader in any group is always, first and foremost, one of communicating what has to be achieved, then deciding on the distribution of the workload, decision-making responsibility and rewards. An integrated approach to this role is presented by Adair.

Adair

Adair developed a concept of leadership he called 'action-centred leadership', which recognised that in any group activity three things were happening simultaneously. A task was being performed, a set of people were having to act in an interdependent way and each individual was undergoing a process of learning. The great merit of this concept was that it saw the task, the group and the individual as part of one process which it was the leader's responsibility to integrate. In this concept, the leader had three objectives – to achieve the task, to build the team and to develop each individual. Central to the achievement of these objectives is to judge each decision by its effect on the task, on the group and on the individual who has to implement it. Figure 7.3 illustrates the concept.

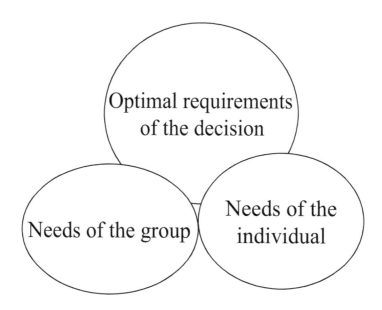

Figure 7.3 Action-centred leadership (J. Adair)

PEOPLE AT WORK

Like other good ideas, 'action-centred leadership' has a simplicity which is not contradicted by psychological theory. It has the additional merit of becoming a 'good habit' in a wide range of personality types. It gets easier with practice.

Although the role of the leader is always concerned with setting objectives and distributing resources, the task of team building – that is, getting the common identity of the group to serve the productive aim of the group – is made harder but is perhaps more crucial in particular circumstances, such as:

- when attachment to the group is involuntary and weak;
- the task of the group is actually an individualistic one;
- there is structured competition within the group;
- the group is not socially homogeneous.

The task is made easier if:

- attachment is strong;
- the task is a group task;
- there are personal characteristics that the group has in common; for example, all females, all same age, all students etc.

We cannot do much about social group formation, but certainly the pay system and the work system should be in harmony.

Further reading

Adair, J. (1984) *Action-Centred Leadership,* London: McGraw-Hill.
Why read this? Straightforward, loaded with wisdom and common sense; what's not to like?
Turner, M.E. and Pratkanis, A.R. (1998) 'Twenty-five years of groupthink theory and research: lessons from the evaluation of a theory', *Organizational Behavior & Human Decision Processes,* 73, 2–3: 105–115.
Why read this? Here is serious material on what one might call the dark side of group behaviour – that capacity of group attachment to be so powerful that individuals cease to think for themselves and follow the group line. In Chapter 2 we looked at mind-sets; this is a similar idea. It can be positively correlated with group performance but stifles individuality and innovation.

CHAPTER

8 Understanding attitudes

Why learn about attitudes?

What should a manager know about attitudes? This is not an easy question to answer, except to say that they should know enough psychology to be able to distinguish between attitudes and opinions, to know the limitations on how far a perceived attitude indicates motivation and to understand that if an attitude survey is required it should be designed by professionals. That said, the sensitive manager looking for clues on employee behaviour knows at least that attitudes are often conspicuous to those who wish to listen and look out for them. This may be helpful in building up a picture of an individual or group.

Chapter objectives

- to define an attitude and to distinguish it from other psychological entities;
- to look at how attitudes are formed;
- to understand the functions of an attitude;
- to understand how attitudes can be changed.

Whilst managing people can be complicated, at least one aspect of human psychology is fairly conspicuous – attitudes. They have entered the daily discourse of managing. You hear references to them every day. A manager reflects: 'selection skills are one thing, but give me the person with the right attitude'. A manager senses things are not quite right with the workforce: 'right now we could do with an attitude survey'. Even American slang has entered the language in the form of '... the problem with him is that he's got attitude', meaning, of course, a bad attitude. In a sense, there is good and bad news here because the fact that attitudes are talked about illustrates their defining quality – that is, that they are positive or negative, but being conspicuous it is too easy for others, in this case managers, to generalise the overall personality from the apparent attitude. This is the bad news because attitudes are more complicated and more important than simple guides to employees' personalities.

PEOPLE AT WORK

People do not walk around with their attitudes printed on T-shirts. We can observe behaviour because it is always there, but attitudes appear only from time to time, to be 'spotted' in the manner of 'bird spotting'. This quality of being 'occasionally visible' is shared with another aspect of human behaviour – the opinion. Consequently, one leads to judgement of the other, and more often than not the two concepts become coterminous. True, people's opinions on matters often betray their attitudes, but that does not mean that attitudes and opinions are the same thing. They are two distinguishable concepts. This often leads to confusion in survey work when it is not clear whether the survey is measuring attitudes or opinions. Although close cousins, they are different and must be measured differently. Whilst this problem is sometimes awkward, it is reasonably easy to solve. The real problem for attitudes is their relationship to behaviour.

It would not be unreasonable to suppose that as attitudes have a positive/negative quality then such a quality might be translated into some form of behaviour. In other words, there should be some consistency between people's verbal expressions of their attitudes towards an object and their behaviour towards it. Although such a connection is notoriously complicated, it is an assumption of the advertising industry that such a relationship exists.

In terms of learning objectives, it is essential to separate attitudes from opinions and to accept the complex relationship which attitudes have with behaviour. Demarcation lines between all the concepts involved are of necessity blurred. Clear distinctions rarely occur; therefore, the study of attitudes automatically embraces opinions, values, beliefs and behaviour.

What is an attitude?

Of the many definitions of attitudes, the one quoted below is perhaps the most famous.

> A mental state of readiness, organised through experience, exerting a direct or dynamic influence upon an individual's response to all objects and situations to which it is related.

The key words here are 'organised', 'experience' and 'influence'. Attitudes are formed by experience and organised in a coherent way within the self. They are also involved in action. Exactly how they get involved in action is complicated, but the connection is nevertheless there. The idea of attitudes as states of readiness is shown by another definition.

> A predisposed response to situations, objects, people, other self-defined areas of life. It has both a perceptual and an affective component. The latter produces a direction in the attitude – positive or negative. This, in turn can influence the perceptual element – we see what we want to see!

UNDERSTANDING ATTITUDES

Unlike the first definition, this one draws out the elements of feeling and evaluation attached to attitudes and invests them with the power to influence how we see things; the 'love is blind' syndrome.

Neither of these definitions gets across those characteristics of an attitude that distinguishes it from other aspects of human psychology, particularly opinions. The key characteristics of an attitude are firstly focus and *fixity*. In other words, attitudes tend to be focused on an object, a person, groups, specific behaviour and particular ideas. They also tend to be fairly fixed over time. This is not to say that they are permanent or that they cannot be changed: they can. However, evidence suggests that they are fairly stable in the short and medium term. Secondly, they are closely related to *feelings*, whereas opinions may or may not carry annotations of feeling. Thirdly, they *live in groups*. What this means is that some aspects of being human are organised in a coherent way within the self. To carry positive and negative components which may be contradictory – for example, to be liberal and conservative about the same issue – is inconsistent and will cause dissonance. The more likely pattern, within the self, would be that someone with, say, a positive attitude towards personal fitness would also be positive about healthy eating, a clean environment, no smoking etc. In other words, there are rope bridges between specific attitudes which join them together in a coherent way. The sense of wholeness and identity depends on our inner coherence.

If anything is 'fixed' in life we tend to assume it is anchored to something. This is true of attitudes. The fixity we associate with attitudes comes from anchors and reinforcers. Obviously, a person does not go around thinking of a particular object. No object is in constant focus; therefore, if the attitude is anchored, the anchor must be broader, deeper and wider than a fleeting focus on an object.

To what is an attitude anchored?

- To values – what is desirable and meaningful across a range of life situations and over time.
- To culture – shared values, shared norms, shared understanding of symbols.
- To habitual behaviour.
- To approved behaviour.

If values, culture and behaviour anchor and reinforce attitudes, the question that arises is: where is an attitude anchored? Tied to a tree like a horse? In a way, yes. The clue comes from the second definition quoted. The perceptual element of attitudes suggests that the attitude is anchored in perceptual categories. If, for one moment, the mind can be envisaged as a set of lockup garages with some we have forgotten we own, some we cannot remember what they contain but some we find useful, it is likely, then, that some lockups contain stuff we like and other lock-ups contain stuff we don't like.

PEOPLE AT WORK

In other words, our perceptual categories have already been evaluated – things we like, things we don't like. It is this quality of positive-negative within our 'way of seeing' that transfers itself to the attitude and is itself reaffirmed by the positive-negative character of the attitude. Most people have an idea of the kind of people they like – a category that has characteristics attached to it. The message from the attitude-perception relationship is that to change an attitude you have to change the way the object is seen, which is the same thing as changing the way the object is categorised – moving it to another lock-up. This is why 'first impressions count' at a selection interview. The selectors will categorise the interviewee, who must ensure that they are seen in the way they wish to be seen.

The character of attitudes

- They are related to an object, a person, an idea, a particular piece of behaviour within the individual's environment.
- They influence perception by influencing the way the individual collects information. In turn, this relationship becomes reciprocal.
- They influence the formation of goals.
- They are learnt and endure.
- They imply both evaluation and feeling.

To understand these characteristics, we need to look at three significant components of an attitude which give it a sense of place, relate it to action and contain a drive in terms of whether an object (including a person) is liked or disliked.

The cognitive component

This component is concerned with the object in terms of attention to it, awareness of it, learning about it, understanding it and placing it in relation to other things. The words we associate with this component are concerned with understanding the object's origins, location and consequences. For example:

Will lead to	causes
Goes with	yields
Comes from	produces
Results in	costs
	prevents

The tone of this component is 'do I understand it'.

The behavioural component

This component is concerned with the action implicit in the perception of the object and sees the object in terms of behaviour, intention, action or inaction. The words we associate with the component are verbs; for example, buy, sell, hit, vote for, kill, rent to, endorse, hire, fire, choose, reject. The tone is 'do I need to do something?'

The affective component

This component is concerned with the object in terms of interest in, evaluation of, feelings towards, belief in etc. The words we associate with this component are, for example, like, dislike, love, hate, want, fear, happy, sad, angry, bored. The tone is, like it don't like it.

Summary

Clearly, the relationship between these components is not one of constant equal influence. The relative dominance of each will change according to these circumstances:

- how much the person already knows about the object;
- whether or not the person can clearly identify the object;
- how much interest the person has in the object.

Forming and maintaining attitudes

Attitudes are learnt – babies don't have attitudes! They are learnt by absorbing the culture, through experiences and through our own behaviour. Although they are personal, they are not determined entirely by the individual. Not only are attitudes learnt, they are also conditioned by the acceptance or rejection of other people the individual regards as important. This may be society itself, a group or simply 'people we like'. This conditioning of attitudes is known as the influence of 'social norm'.

Because they are personal, attitudes perform certain *functions* for the individual, such as:

- they direct people; moving from the undesirable to the desirable;
- they help to define who we are;
- they give direction to experience. We have learnt something and our attitudes tell us what to do when the experience is repeated.

Attitudes have two distinct relationships with behaviour. It would be wonderful if we could predict behaviour from attitudes but alas this is not really possible. However, if the notion of *intention to behave* is placed between attitudes and behaviour, then careful measurement can produce some predictions.

78 PEOPLE AT WORK

A more intimate bond between attitudes and behaviour can be expressed in the conundrum 'Do I behave a certain way because of my attitudes or is my attitude an after-the-fact justification for my behaviour?' Both are true.

If we habitually perform certain behaviour, then we take on the appropriate attitude. On the other hand, if we hold an attitude rooted in some personal value and are confronted with the need to respond to some stimulus, then we are likely to follow our attitude and behave accordingly.

Attitudes run in packs

Like wolves, attitudes run in packs. The great advantage of this is that to find and measure an attitude you begin by rounding up 'known associates' rather in the manner of the police. In fact, the idea of 'running in packs' is a rather flippant expression of the psychological conditions of concept, organisation and of 'consistency'. The need to be consistent within ourselves. It is this need for consistency that is so helpful because the discovery of one attitude may lead to the discovery of others. In fact this relationship between attitudes is one of ever greater parameters so that each attitude is subsumed within a larger one.

In other words, each attitude group belongs to a larger attitude group or construct, thus forming a hierarchical basis for 'internal organisation'. For example the attitude 'I hate sport' may be associated with physical laziness or a preference for artistic pursuits and be subsumed within some larger constraints such as 'a dislike of competition', 'strong individualism' or 'a dislike of being in teams'. There are many ways in which one attitude can be interpreted, and it is the task of attitude measurement to find the attitude under investigation through the manipulation of assumed known associates and assumed larger constructs. A further example may help to make the idea clear.

If the object of an attitude study is 'people's attitudes towards a half bottle of wine', then a sample of wine drinkers would be used in the study. To create a survey, the researcher would need to have in mind two artificial 'ideal types'. Characteristics of people who would be in favour of half bottles of wine and characteristics of those who would be negative towards the poor half bottle! The suggested 'ideal type' below uses constructs that are far wider than mere 'drinking habits'.

Positive	Negative
Moderate in all consumption	Indulgent
Concern for drink driving	Thoughtless about drink driving
Separates business and pleasure	Mixes business and pleasure
Concern for health	Not very concerned about health

Whether these concepts actually represent the attitude to the object can only be proved by testing.

Changing attitudes

The objectives of this chapter have been to understand attitudes and to show how they are focused entities; one always has an attitude towards something. That something is salient to understanding how attitudes can be changed. Change is all about seeing the object differently, and from management's point of view that means involving new knowledge. Do something differently and you begin to see it differently. There is an important paradigm for attitude change, which is:

- if attitudes are fixed by their anchors – other attitudes, values, behaviour, cognitive categories

  THEN

- to change an attitude means attacking one or all of the anchors. The key is to find out how far it is based on knowledge, feeling or habit.

To be more specific, attitude change means:

- moving an attitude from one perceptual category to another;
- if the new attitude is not buried in another category it is not internalised!
- The intervening factor is new information;
- the re-enforcing factor is new behaviour, which is why role change is at the heart of attitude change.

Remember that attitudes can easily be confused with motivation – that person has a bad attitude or a good attitude. The object here is 'work'. Seen as a motivational issue, the approach may be incentives or sanctions, but seen as an attitudinal issue, the answer may lie in changing the role and invoking new knowledge to be learned.

Attitudes are amongst the easiest of psychological entities to measure; however, the techniques involved are beyond the scope of this book. You should always seek professional assistance.

Further reading

Rajecki, D.W. (1990) *Attitudes*, Sunderland, MA: Sinauer Associates Publishers, Unit 1 The Conceptualization of psychological attitudes, pp. 1–38.

Why read this? The quotes above come from the work of Allport (1935) and this book explores Allport's definitions in a way that reveals their

80 PEOPLE AT WORK

importance to understanding and to measurement. These definitions have stood the test of time and are the bedrock of modern thinking about attitudes.

Clark, M.A., Riley, M.J., Wilkie, E. and Wood, R.C. (1998) *Researching and Writing Dissertations in Hospitality and Tourism Management,* London: International Thomson Business Press, p. 281.

Why read this? It contains some specific measurement methods that apply to attitudes in the context of hospitality.

CHAPTER

9 Identity and diversity

In human resource management, we cannot ignore the need to manage diversity; individual and group differences matter. Whether at one-to-one or policy level, there are behavioural implications which need to be addressed. In society, the word diversity is commonly associated with demographics such as age, gender, race and religion. What drives policy in this area is the need for fair and equal treatment and the need to avoid discrimination. When we take these issues into the workplace, we see the underlying psychological force that causes us to address diversity and discrimination; the search for identity.

Chapter objectives

- to understand the concept of self-identity;
- to understand the relationship of identity to group behaviour;
- to introduce the many forms of identity;
- to understand the policy issues that impact on diversity.

In modern thinking about motivation, it has been realised that people behave in accordance with how they define themselves as well as by trying to meet their psychological needs. Identity is about the inner sense of self. Not, it must be emphasised, your personality traits (e.g. introvert-extrovert) but how you describe yourself to yourself (self-identity; e.g. I'm a hard-working generous kind of person) and how that self-identity is constructed through the social contexts you live in (social identity; e.g. I'm a conservative; I'm a sports fan). What is important is that the personal and the social are inseparable. Together they produce yet another layer of individual differences and an individual pattern of group association which leads to loyalties and biases. Hence, the problem of managing diversity is about managing individuals whose identity matters to their behaviour – what we might call identity-sensitive behaviour. And, it is about managing groups whose behaviour is driven by their identity. Diversity is not really an issue unless people behave in terms of their identity or identities, but they inevitably do.

The hospitality context

Think of all the differences between occupational groups within hospitality; the uniforms, the multinational workforce, national identity groups, the languages and the age groups. Hospitality is an industry where the skilled and the unskilled work together and where each is dependent on the other. This is an unusual technological process; often the skilled are separated from the unskilled or semi-skilled workers – not in hospitality. What this means in practice is, firstly, that clearly differentiated groups have to work together; and secondly, that any universal policy, such as a percentage pay rise across the whole workforce, may be seen and felt differentially by different groups. What one group considers fair may not be shared by another – yet they work in a mutually dependent system.

What is self-identity?

Self-identity is your personal identity which you curate for yourself out of your view of the world and the associations you have with groups.

- Self-identity is how you describe yourself to yourself; not in terms of personality traits but in terms of how you place yourself within your own world view.
- We all have multiple identities, a family, a profession, a political leaning etc. They are constructed through group affiliation (social identity).

How does self-identity come out of social identity?

Self-identity is essentially a conscious sense of individual uniqueness which contains an unconscious striving for continuity and a feeling of belonging to some group or groups to which they are attached. We do not remake ourselves every morning. Group attachment forms the basis of our social identity; it is a person's definition of self in terms of some social group membership with the associated value connotations and emotional significance. It is not necessary to be an actual member of a group; the connection could be purely through associations in the mind. One could see oneself as a feminist or a liberal without joining a feminist group or a political party.

The key theoretical basis is Social Identity Theory. The theory proposes a process whereby people come to identify with particular groups and separate themselves from others. That is the behavioural implication that draws our attention to discrimination. The way in which people identify with social categories shapes how they perceive the immediate social context and how they are prepared to act within that perceived context. It also holds that contrasts between social categories serve an important function. We are familiar with intergroup behaviour from Chapter 7, with its emphasis on identity

IDENTITY AND DIVERSITY

based on attachment to groups and the behaviour this engenders. It is easy to fall into the trap of seeing discrimination in pejorative terms. This is not necessarily the case; knowing where you stand in relation to others is important and allows you to navigate through social circumstances. However, the discrimination implied by our group favouritism does carry the potential for intergroup conflict. The strength and the emotional attachment that clings to a group increases when the group is homogeneous, when it is the sole group of members, when it is in competition with other groups and when there is a clear out-group. This is a platform for a strong identity.

The case of multiple identities

Everything becomes more complicated by the fact that individuals can have multiple identities which stem from different group influences, all of which can influence behaviour. Figure 9.1 shows the range of social influence.

On the face of it, this seems to create an insolvable puzzle for management: which identity is causing what behaviour? If we look at the ideas of identity and diversity together, we see that essentially management has two issues to address. Firstly, to recognise that *identity matters to behaviour*. For example, skilled chefs see themselves as just that – skilled team workers identifying with a profession and with a brigade. Secondly, groups within hospitality have separate identities and see each other's worth differentially. The priority of housekeeping is to provide clean rooms, but reception want them at

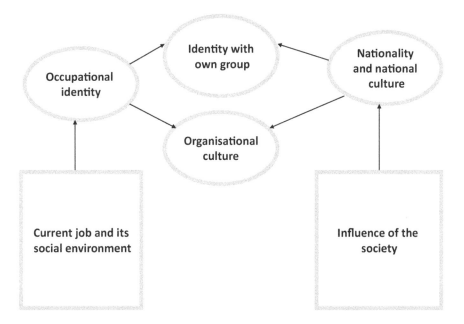

Figure 9.1 Multiple influences on personal identity

PEOPLE AT WORK

the moment the new guest arrives. There is structured potential conflict here which both groups have to live with comfortably.

Whatever the problems, Figure 9.1 also illustrates that some of the influences are within management's range to exert influence and therefore are possible solutions – the occupation, the work group and the organisation's culture and reputation. Appreciating skill, encouraging teamwork and having a good reputation in the labour market are a platform for getting individuals to harmonise their personal identity with that of the organisation; in other words, making organisational identity the primary one – this the strategic repose for avoiding conflict and countering discrimination.

HRM policy issues that impact on identity and diversity

Lying at the heart of diversity management is avoiding employees having feelings of inequality and a sense of being discriminated against. The obvious areas of concern are pay structures and opportunity structures. There will always be legitimate, rational and technical reasons why some occupations and some people get more pay than others. The word legitimate is crucial here because diversity management is about ensuring that differentials between occupational groups and individuals are accepted by the whole workforce. The hospitality industry sees many pay differentials as being legitimised by tradition. Whilst true, it is unwise to assume that this can persist. The notion of 'acceptable' means that the differentials cannot be a source of intergroup conflict. What is never legitimate is for some groups or individuals to be excluded from access to opportunities and therefore from higher earnings. The hospitality industry is one in which for most occupations skills can be accumulated fairly quickly, making strict hiring criteria less daunting for the ambitious.Higher than average upward mobility is a feature of the industry. However, the constant use of the subjective 'merit' as a criterion for promotion makes real opportunity seem more ambiguous to applicants.

Policy areas that impact on diversity

Pay differentials. Pay differentials need to be reviewed and validated regularly. Labour turnover is one indicator of problems in this area. Pay levels tend to be regulated by market forces, but that does not excuse tolerating internal problems caused by inequity.

Access. Successful diversity management has an underlying driver and that is development. Having promotion and learning policies that are open and encouraged by management is the ideal platform for development. For employees to see that everyone has a chance at improvement is good for morale. The facility to transfer occupations and departments creates a fluid environment that supports diversity.

Tapping resources. Making use of what human resources you have rather than always searching the labour market gives the organisation a reputation for being a good employer.

Collaborative. Where appropriate, encourage collaborative activity.

Managing change. Being careful to communicate change and to realise that when a job changes relationships change at the same time. Think action-centred leadership (Chapter 7).

Do not neglect casual labour. Casual labour is a crucial resource in hospitality and a direct link to the external labour market. Having a clear policy about valuing and retaining this workforce is important because it comes into regular contact with permanent staff.

It is very easy for concerns about discrimination to be swallowed up by the attractive ambience created by the kind of multicultural workforces we often find in hospitality – all those different nationalities and all that diversity. A colourful scenario; no problem here then! Not true, it must not be forgotten that identity is essentially a personal construct, and people alter their behaviour to match their self-identity; theory suggests this can be translated into group behaviour.

Further reading

Shen, J., Chanda, A. and D'Netto, B. (2009) 'Managing diversity through human resource management: an international perspective and conceptual framework', *The International Journal of Human Resource Management*, 20, 2: 235–251.

Why read this? They make an incredibly important point about diversity management in that HRM can spend all its time on compliance with laws and equality policies and fail to take advantage of the very diversity of a workforce and see what developing that diversity can bring to an organisation.

CHAPTER

10 Organisations and authority

We have made many references in the previous chapters to 'the context' of decision-making, of communication, of knowledge; that context is, of course, the organisation you work in. The organisation becomes more than a context, a background when you assume a managerial role and automatically take on personal authority. Once anyone takes on the role of manager, they assume authority. Like putting on a coat, they suddenly find they have an additional quality. At first it may not fit too easily, but with experience it becomes more comfortable. If we were to look for some central or pivotal idea which formed the very heart of understanding management we would probably find two things – profit and authority. Our concern here is with authority – the right to give orders and command obedience. Authority owes its pre-eminence to the fact that, first, it is such an intrinsic quality of the 'role' of manager that it becomes part of the psychology of the role incumbent; and second, that it is the very building block of organisation structure. Before exploring authority, we need to appreciate the context – the organisation.

Chapter objectives
- to understand the nature and sources of authority;
- to understand the basic model of bureaucratic organisation;
- to be able to judge hospitality organisations against bureaucratic models;
- to understand normative control.

The individual manager and the organisation

When we think something has worked well we often say, 'it worked like clockwork'. This idea of thinking of organisations as being like a machine is rather an attractive one – cogs and wheels pulling in the same direction. In this modern day world of IT systems, the vision of organisations being machines seems more apposite. Indeed, many such analogies are made in the literature; however, this notion, whilst useful, cannot be stretched too far. A clock is, after all, only telling us a point on an unchanging continuum. A commercial organisation has to deal with ever-changing markets where uncertainty roams. The cogs

ORGANISATIONS AND AUTHORITY   87

and wheels in this case have to be more flexible. Flexibility, in any form, can only come from one source; managerial judgement. Most organisations consist of layers of management, with jobs differentiated by specialist functions. If we ask why this is always the case, we have to think back to first principles. If the task is too big for one person, then the work has to be divided – this is as true for management as it is for workers making a car. Here we revert to the ideas in Chapters 1 and 2. Managers have to make decisions and no one person can do everything, and for any one managerial role there are limits set by the principle of *bounded rationality* – the limits of individual knowledge. When the information needed to make a decision from a set of alternatives is too large to predict consequences, then the job is too big for anyone. Hence, we need the division of labour of management work – that is, we form an organisation. Here we are joining together the ideas of managerial capacity and organisation.

The bureaucratic model

Normally when we analyse organisation, the starting point is bureaucracy, particularly the standard model which decrees strict adherence to rules and where authority is vested only in the position not the incumbent. This is what a pure bureaucracy looks like:

- formalised employment relationships;
- clearly defined roles;
- elaborate division of labour;
- centralised yet delegated decision-making;
- hierarchical system of control;
- proliferation of rules;
- an ethos of regularity, predictability and control;
- formal and directive.

There are advantages, such as:

- centralisation leads to a consistent strategic perspective and clarity of purpose;
- specialisation leads to technical efficiency;
- administrative rules give consistency of justice;
- control is simplified;
- accountability within the organisation is transparent;
- maintained by secure career structures.

Against these we have to consider the disadvantages:

- centralisation leads to remoteness and lack of involvement;
- specialisation and formal hierarchy make it difficult to change the structure – therefore, the organisation cannot easily respond to change;

PEOPLE AT WORK

- specialisation leads to problems of coordination and integration;
- rules do not motivate;
- formal hierarchy means slow communication;
- standardisation of roles stifles initiative and creativity.

This comparative analysis is compounded by the rise of information technology, which with its ability to specify and measure clearly leans heavily towards bureaucracy. It is with a perspective on bureaucracy that we should look at hospitality organisations.

The hospitality context

Whether we have in mind a hotel, a restaurant, a cruise ship or a leisure facility, we are thinking about an entity that is simultaneously both a service provider and a production unit; meals are served, drinks are served whilst food is being cooked and clean rooms are made available. Whilst this is going on, data is being processed in real time. Many different work processes are in action together, each involving a variety of skills and knowledge. All this variety is performed through a division of labour which to be efficient must be systematic but more importantly be able to react to contingency. The demand for services and goods in hospitality is always a contingent demand; when the customer wants something, it is then and only then that the system swings into action. On the face of it, it would seem that if hospitality organisations have to be responsive to contingent demand, then they cannot be bureaucratic! This is only partially true. There are logistics to distribute labour and materials to where they are needed. This requires formal specification and rules so that people know what they are doing. It is the contingent nature of consumer demand that necessitate staff having personal freedom to respond in an appropriate way. No matter what degree of formalisation exists, the systematic view of hospitality operations is not the complete picture. There is the crucial element of quality standards. In effect, only the customer can judge what is 'good' and what is 'clean', yet management have to specify standards and control them. This turns hospitality organisations into normative organisations where because it is hard to specify standards actual performance standards are collectively understood by management and staff. In other words, management have to establish, through example and vigilance, 'norms' that are understood by everybody. The authority of management is, by necessity, visible and active – always vigilant about good practice and the required standards.

The questions we are left with are: how close is the modern hospitality organisation to the bureaucratic model and to what degree can such organisations be managed through normative control? These questions are now explored.

Organisations are not simply the sum of the individual human beings who happen to be employed at a particular time. They are social structures which have goals and purposes, and these structures give people a structured environment into which they bring their own needs, motives and abilities. What is helpful would be to identify the point where the individual meets the organisation, to see clearly who the agent of action is and to place both the organisation and its employees in the same environmental context.

Where the organisation as an independent entity and the individual actually meet is in the concept of *role*. The prescribed role is where the organisation inputs to the individual its goals and purposes whilst simultaneously the individual brings to the role their own goals, motives and needs. The interaction of these two perspectives within the role, in aggregate, results in what we call organisational behaviour. Organisations take action: they make things, they provide services and nothing works without leadership and an organising force; this is the role of management. They accomplish their role by having and applying *authority*. So what is authority?

Managerial authority

Perception of authority

It is not unusual for those taking on authority for the first time to find themselves feeling uncomfortable. This feeling is engendered by the presence of a difficult question – how do you know when your authority is working? The answer is by the way your orders are received and carried out by your subordinates. Everything is conditional and a matter of degree, and it takes experience to judge when things are going well. Coterminous with the concept of authority is the idea of legitimacy – that is, the notion that your right to give orders is regarded as proper and acceptable by those who are on the receiving end. Legitimacy, like authority, simultaneously exists at a general level and rests on specific acts. Thus, in the employee's mind there is a view of management in general and individual managers in particular. To simplify the argument:

1. employees may accept management's authority in general, but object or withdraw legitimacy on particular acts of authority – 'I'll do anything you ask, but not that ...';
2. some managers will have stronger authority than others in the sense that they will be regarded as more legitimate – 'I'll do that for her, but not for you!';
3. the legitimacy of authority is related to the source of that authority as seen by the employee. Consequently, there will be different ways of legitimising authority.

PEOPLE AT WORK

It is reasonable to assume that not all orders are perceived as either a reward or a threat; some will simply be obeyed without feeling. It is also not difficult to imagine that within one organisation some managers will find it easier than others to command respect and obedience and that any one manager may be perceived in different ways by different individuals.

What really matters is that managers have the respect of their employees. It is still, however, worthwhile considering the various bases of authority. Any manager's authority springs from many sources simultaneously, including:

- responsibility;
- personality;
- right of 'office';
- type of knowledge or expertise;
- knowledge differential with subordinates;
- age;
- length of service.

A manager's authority springs from all these sources simultaneously, but what matters is how the individual manager sees their authority. Part of their self-description will include 'why people obey my orders'. It may well be that one of the sources is favoured in this self-description. In a similar manner, as authority requires legitimacy, subordinates will have a perception of what that manager's authority is based on and will judge their behaviour according to that. In other words, it is the employees' judgement of the manager's competence that causes respect or derision. An example would be appropriate. Suppose a manager defines him- or herself as being highly managerially trained with a set of skills unique to managers. Subordinates, however, see this particular manager's authority as coming from the 'office' and backed up by organisation rules. Here, the assumptions about authority are not mutual. Does it matter? The answer to this question is yes and no.

Examples can be found to suit both cases. Often assumptions about authority are culturally derived – the hospitality industry would be an example where workers assume that managers have technical knowledge of the job workers do. Other industrial workers might be amazed if they found out that managers could do their job, expecting them to know only about management. What is clear is that demonstrated competence can override any difficulties that may arise from lack of mutuality over perceptions of authority.

Five points need to be made about the importance of managers' self-perceptions of authority and workers' perceptions of authority.

1. Perceptions can change over time.
2. Perceptions of authority matter in relationships and form the basis of obedience.
3. Demonstrable competence can override any contradictions between managers' perceptions and the workers' view.
4. The manager's self-perception of anything will change as they rise up the organisation hierarchy.

ORGANISATIONS AND AUTHORITY 91

5. The manager's perception of authority will be influenced by the form of authority embedded in the organisation structure.

Everything so far has been concerned with sources of management authority as if authority only resided in management. This is true only in the legal sense – other sources of authority, legitimate or otherwise, are always at large and include:

- employee autonomy;
- tradition;
- the status quo;
- precedent.

You cannot have it both ways. If either the job cannot be totally formally controlled or you deliberately ask a worker to take some responsibility for their work, then you must expect them to grant themselves authority over it. The consequence of granting autonomy to a worker is that you grant authority as well. If, as in the hospitality industry, service occupation standards are in the hands of the servers, then conscientiousness is essential. This can only spring from trust on your part and a sense of responsibility on the part of the employee. The formation of an occupational identity and pride in work is based on the individual taking responsibility for their work. Not surprisingly, this can lead to clashes between the authority of managers and that of workers. Two susceptible areas are standard of output and technological substitution. In the first case, it would be more difficult for managers to try to change standards if they did not know how to do the work themselves – an area where perceptions of authority really count.

Not only can workers claim authority over their own work but situations have authority as well. The status quo – how we have always done things around here – has its own authority because it has a self-justifying rationale. People feel comfortable and are not threatened by the status quo. A slightly different case is that of 'tradition'. This implies both a value and an ideal which is worth continuing from the past. The word traditional cannot really be used to justify something except when it is describing some activity which is valued. The authority of tradition lies in the value of whatever it is maintaining. The status quo need not represent a value at all. In a similar manner, precedent is a justification only when it is linked to some value like fairness or equity. In the hotel and catering industry, standards can become traditional values; when challenged by economics they can be defended only on the grounds of being appreciated by customers.

The central point here is that these alternative sources of authority present managers with a challenge when they wish to make changes.

Authority and organisational structure

This last point leads us towards the question of the relationship between authority, as a concept, and organisational structure. Organisations consist

PEOPLE AT WORK

of sets of 'roles', each with areas of responsibility and authority. These roles are normally arranged in a hierarchy, and the whole purpose of the edifice is to exercise control over the activities of the organisation. The organising principle behind the division of labour, both vertically and horizontally, is functional rationality, by which is meant dividing work groups up by clearly different production or service activities – e.g. kitchen is separated from restaurant services which are separated from room cleaning. These activities must be controlled, and there are three broad forms of such control. First, the form of control could be technical, based on the control of output; or second, bureaucratic, based on rules. The motto of the former would be the 'best way to do things' and the latter would be the 'proper way to do things'. Earlier we discussed some limitations on technical and bureaucratic control and therefore the third possibility is normative control, which places a greater burden on 'ideals and standards' as the basis of control – 'the way things should be done'.

The point being made here is that different forms of control require different sources of authority. If the form of control is bureaucratic, based on rules, then the form of authority would stem from 'the office' rather than any characteristics of the person holding the office. In such a bureaucratic structure role, incumbents are merely administering rules. If the form of control is technical, then this too could form the basis of a bureaucratic structure, but it is more likely to be one in which the authority basis is technical knowledge differentials. The greater the degree of scope and authority granted to a role, the more likely it is that the source of authority will be personality and knowledge. A charismatic leader does not rely on 'position' and 'structure' as the source of their authority but on their own will. There is often a succession problem in roles which use personality as a basis of authority. Rarely does the successor exactly match the outgoing incumbent. Replacing Caesar has always been a problem!

One of the most striking characteristics of the hospitality industry is that the rapid turnover of business requires strict formal financial controls, but the actual activities that represent that business are very hard to formally control. As long as consumer demand fluctuates, and there are individual differences in performance, this will always be so. For this reason, the industry tends to have a combination of formal control mechanisms and fairly rigid role descriptions, which give it the look of a bureaucracy while at the same time having a structure which copes with all this variation and subjectivity through personal authority and leadership. This appears to the outsider to be very ad hoc.

Power and authority

If authority is a 'right' conferred by a number of sources, is that any different from having power? The two concepts are inseparable, but it is important to

ORGANISATIONS AND AUTHORITY   93

Table 10.1 Types of power

Type of power	Applied by
Physical	Force
Resource	Exchange and bargaining
Position	Rules
Expert	Knowledge differential and learning opportunities
Personal	Persuasion

try to distinguish them. A common classification of types of power would be as shown in Table 10.1.

This classification could just as easily be about sources of authority. The way to distinguish between them is to see authority as a 'right to give orders' and power in terms of sanctions and rewards which are a contingent necessity. Rules of discipline and bargaining strength, for example, come from the same knapsack – they are both power 'tools' and can be used as rewards or sanctions.

The difference between power and authority can best be seen by what they share – both require to be legitimised but in different ways. Acts of power will be judged by 'that is fair or not fair' whereas the reaction to authority is 'you can/cannot do that to me'. To go further, authority and power have a different relationship to responsibility. If responsibility confers authority by conferring the right to decide, it does not automatically confer the use of any sanctions or rewards. While an area of responsibility justifies authority, power can be justified only 'in usage' and in terms of fairness and necessity. It is the idea that power is judged by how it is used, rather than by its existence, that brings the two concepts back together again. Clearly, if power is seen to be constantly misused, or blatantly unfair, then subordinates will begin to question the authority of the user of power. The less legitimate your authority is, the more you may need to use power, which only undermines your authority still more. It is a cycle which is all too easy to get into.

Authority and communication

It was suggested in Chapter 3 that all management behaviour communicates by sending signals to subordinates. This was particularly so, the argument went, when standards were subjective. If the manager failed to see low standards this might be interpreted by subordinates as the manager not caring. This idea of signals is important because it reminds us that everything managers do is connected to the perceptions of their authority and that not all communication is written or oral or even deliberate.

It is a universal tenet of management that 'good' communication is a good thing. Like not kicking the cat, it is something hard to disagree with. Good

94 PEOPLE AT WORK

communication is usually seen as clear communication. The merit of clarity is usually seen as giving the recipient of the communication a clear unambiguous understanding of what is required. Exactly, but the argument stops too soon. If we go on, then a connection appears between clarity of communication and perceptions of authority. *Regular* clear communication results in:

- employees understand what you want and why you want it;
- employees realise that you know what you want;
- employees see continuity in your instructions;
- employees begin to understand your logic and feel more comfortable with your authority because it cannot spring surprises;
- employees understand what you stand for.

In other words, the message here is that clarity increases the legitimacy of your authority and consequently the respect you are given because regular unambiguous communication encourages the employee to adjust their assumptions of what is expected of them.

Further reading

Bushard, S.C., Glascoff, D.W., Doty, D.H., Frank, M. and Burke, F. (2010) 'Delegation, authority and responsibility: a reconfiguration of an old paradigm', *Advances in Management*, 3, 9: 9–12.

Why read this? This paper confronts what we take for granted in terms of how responsibility forms the bedrock of authority and what delegation actually means.

PART III

The economics of labour in hospitality

CHAPTER

11 Economics of labour in hospitality

It is probably a good idea to look at the basics of hospitality economics before going into the economics of labour for that industry. In fundamental terms, the economics of hotels is that of buildings: property. Consequently, in the case of transient residential buildings, which are what hotels are, the relevant economic concept is asset management and land value.However, in terms of operational economics – that is, how the building makes money – the relevant concept is that of throughput – getting people to visit and stay. This is the economics of room occupancy and food and beverage turnover. Both asset value and throughput estimate come together in the planning of hotel development – what does it cost and what is the expected level of business? This broad statement of affairs applies not just to hotels but any asset-founded entity in the wider hospitality industry – a cruise ship, a restaurant, a bar, a pub, a coffee house, even a sandwich shop. They are all governed by asset price and by throughput economics. Our question is where does the economics of labour fit in?

Chapter objectives

The aim of this chapter is to use economic theory to give you some concepts that will help you to understand how hospitality labour markets work and how its occupations are valued and priced. You will understand:

- the nature of work in hospitality and what that means for labour markets;
- the crucial role of uncertainty in labour pricing;
- the difference between internal and external labour markets;
- the way in which the nature of a job foretells the market it exists in.

Two fundamental assumptions

In one sense, the ergonomic design of the hospitality asset will determine how it is staffed, but for the most part, labour economics is concerned with anticipating and reacting to consumer demand. In other words, the amount of labour consumed by any hospitality establishment is determined by the

THE ECONOMICS OF LABOUR IN HOSPITALITY

quality of product and service it sets out to offer and, most importantly, by the variations in throughput demanded by the consumer market. We can conclude, therefore, that a large element of labour, to put it in economic terms, is a variable factor of production.

It is fortunate that for our understanding of the economics of labour for hospitality that we are guided by some common features of the nature of work and of consumption. These features lead us to make two safe assumptions. The first is that most of the knowledge and skill used in hospitality jobs are easy to acquire. They can be learnt fairly quickly with simple instruction on the job. This means that recruitment is always from the large general unskilled labour market. Economists call this the secondary labour market. We have to take a breath here to avoid falling into a trap of thinking that job attributes that are easy to acquire must be unskilled. This is not always the case because skill is a slippery concept to define and label onto jobs. Whilst it is undoubtedly true that many jobs in hospitality are unskilled manual labour, some of those jobs have elements of discretion, timing, contextual knowledge and multi-tasking attached to them. One must be careful when throwing the word unskilled around. Anyone can carry two plates to a table, but to coordinate timing with guest demeanour and a busy kitchen requires some system knowledge, social skill and possibly language knowledge. Cooking for your family does not mean sharing the same skill set as a chef feeding over a hundred people. Scale itself imposes different motor skills, timing and product and system knowledge. From the outside, the business of labelling hospitality jobs is complicated, but it becomes a little clearer from inside the industry when the quality of the establishment is applied. We know something about a cook when he or she is working in a five-star establishment – they are skilled. From within the hospitality industry we make relative judgements about levels of skill.

Our second assumption concerns consumers of hospitality services, and here we are back with that important convention – throughput. There will always be variation in demand for hospitality, which means there is always uncertainty. Tourism is well acquainted with issues of seasonality, but variations in demand go much deeper and are much finer at the establishment level. Forecasting demand is not an exact science, and at street level footfall it is even less predictable. This phenomenon of variation creates in the minds of managers uncertainty, and their strategic response to this is to make as many factors of production as possible variable and to constantly reduce their cost. Labour is perhaps the most significant variable cost; therefore, manning levels and pay becomes a primary focus of control. We can see clearly that it is the uncertainty of demand that is the primary deflationary pressure on hospitality pay. At this point it is necessary to point to another trap – which is so easy to fall into – and that is equating unskilled with unproductive. It will be shown in a later chapter that in an industry where the demand for labour is direct – that is, required for what it can produce rather than what a machine can produce – it is the work of unskilled labour that gives hospitality establishments their productivity.

ECONOMICS OF LABOUR IN HOSPITALITY **99**

What follows from both the assumptions of ease of skill acquisition and of uncertain consumer demand is that hospitality labour is low-paid work. Again we must take a breath. Whilst it is true that even in countries where tourism is the main industry wages in that industry are below national averages, it is equally true that there are many high-skilled jobs and many high-paying jobs; by inference the distinction indicates that there are also low- skilled high-paid jobs! It is complicated.

How labour markets work

All organisations live in a labour market environment; it is the sea on which they sail. To complain about the labour market is like the captain of a ship complaining about the sea. Yet labour markets are invariably problematic to organisations because they are mostly invisible things. In order to make sense of the chapter on hotel and catering labour markets, it is necessary to look first at some basic ideas and concepts that appertain to understanding labour markets.

Labour markets exist on two levels; factual and perceptual. At any one time, people will be seeking employment or trying to change their jobs. Simultaneously, employers will be seeking new employees. Wage rates will be set, recruitment policies implemented, people will need training and people will have to move. This is the daily life of labour markets. Thousands of independent decisions made by employers and employees make up the trends in mobility, the surpluses of or shortages of supply and the excesses or lack of demand. In other words, whatever the state of supply and demand in a labour market, it is brought about by the independent and unconnected decisions of thousands of people.

According to conventional economic theory, supply and demand will be brought into equilibrium by the price of labour – i.e. the rate of pay. However, behind the assumption of a perfect market is a perfect flow of information between buyers and sellers of labour. In a perfect world, the buyers would know how many people have the skills they desire, how many would like to learn them and where these people are. Conversely, people would know how many vacancies there are, in what organisations and at what rate of pay.

Labour markets run on information, but they are invariably less than perfect mechanisms. What both buyers and sellers are left with are their perceptions and assumptions of supply and demand. We may think that there is no current demand for our skills, yet it may be that there is! An employer may think it is going to be easy to recruit a certain skill and set the rate accordingly but may find that it is not. In the absence of perfect information and measurement, trial and error is both the decision process and a learning source.

While it is difficult to know a labour market, learning about it is a matter of reading signals in society such as the general level of employment, education trends and major changes in the birth rate. More important, however, is to look closer to home at the local labour market and particularly at the rate

THE ECONOMICS OF LABOUR IN HOSPITALITY

of labour turnover, competitors' pay rates, the number of vacancies and the number of applicants per vacancy. It is also possible to survey local markets in various ways.

As far as the hospitality industry is concerned, there are two aspects of labour market theory that are relevant to understanding the industry's market behaviour. Firstly, what is significant to hospitality management is that labour markets divide into two general sectors: what are called primary and secondary markets. The primary market can be characterised by educational qualifications and stable employment with benefits. It is a small pool divided by specialisations. By contrast, the far larger secondary market is characterised by low qualifications, unskilled jobs and unstable employment conditions. The hospitality industry fishes in both pools for its staff.

The second aspect of theory that is crucial for hospitality managers is that of the internal labour market. How skills and knowledge are allocated within a hospitality establishment in relation to what goes on in the external market is central to our understanding of hospitality labour management. Later in this chapter we will distinguish between the external and the internal labour markets.

It would be wrong to assume that managers do not have any control over the labour market because they do. For a start, although all organisations are involved in the national labour market, what counts to the health of the organisation is the performance of its local labour market and the particular segments of it that are salient. What arbitrates the size of these markets is the degree of specialisation of the organisation. If the skills required are very specific to the organisation, then there is a choice between fishing in a small pond or doing a lot of training. If the skills are generally held in the wider population, then the market will be larger and it is a case of trawling with a large net.

Notwithstanding the size of the labour markets, managers have at their disposal a wide range of tools for meeting the problems of labour markets; e.g. increasing pay, more training, altering hiring standards, promoting from within, plus many more. Increasing pay, for example, might not only attract more people but may do so by extending the geographical limits of the local market by revaluing 'travel to work costs'.

One concept central to labour markets is that of elasticity. It is necessary to understand the economic notion of elasticity. Quite simply, if pay is the driving force of the market, how responsive is the demand for labour to rises and falls in the rate of pay, and how responsive is the supply of labour to rises and falls in the rate of pay? Even casual analysis of hospitality indicates that as the work can easily be learned jobs are open to the large secondary market and therefore are likely to respond quickly to changes in the level of pay. If we were short of brain surgeons, it would take a long time for any increase in pay to attract more people into training for that profession – not so, for a room cleaner.

Labour markets are always an unknown quality, but acceptance of that and a willingness to try to understand what is going on is essential to HRM. All HRM policies, but particularly those relating to recruitment and training, are, to a large extent, dependent on labour market factors.

The supply curve for labour

In order to see how the market prices hospitality jobs, it would be useful to look, in rather simplistic terms, at how individuals supply their labour to the market. What level of pay brings them to the market and into work? Figure 11.1 is a simple illustration which shows that as pay increased people offered more effort in terms of hours of work. What is interesting is that the curve eventually bends backwards for those people offered less hours for more money. If you think of the working day as split between leisure and work and visualise it as completion between them, then there comes a point when a person wants more time for leisure and give less time to work. At first glance it would seem that this idea might apply only to high earners, but there is another argument. If we evoke convenience as an attribute of work where work hours need to meet some personal goals, it might be applicable to part-time, flexible working arrangements.

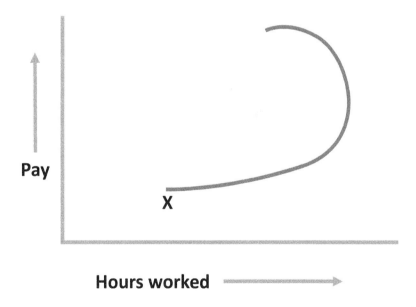

Figure 11.1 Supply curve for labour

THE ECONOMICS OF LABOUR IN HOSPITALITY

What is important for hospitality is the placement of the lower end of the curve – that is, the rate of pay that attracts people to work. In economic terms, the lowest point (X) is often given appropriate labels – subsistence wage, a legal minimum wage or a designated living wage. It need not be any of these, but it is a rate that activates the market. It might be insufficient to attract in a local market, but it may be attractive to another, possibly overseas, market. Hospitality, in its international setting, imports labour because that basic rate is relatively high and therefore attractive to a different market. The conditions which promote mobility are:

- when the absolute value of income does not reach an acceptable level;
- when extended labour supply does not produce an acceptable level of subsistence;
- when community bonds and norms of distribution produce insufficient work and income.

The job foretells the market

There are five broad characteristics of labour markets, and the nature of any job foretells where that job sits within the labour market structures.

1. *Size (large/small)*. Labour markets vary in the number of people they contain. Clearly the principal cause of this would be the level of skill. The more unskilled the work, the larger the market would be.
2. *Status (primary/secondary)*. Strongly related to size, markets are classified into primary and secondary. Primary markets contain good jobs with careers attached and require qualifications to enter. As a consequence, they are more stable. By contrast, secondary markets contain largely unskilled jobs requiring no training. Consequently, such markets are characterised by mobility and variable attachment to the market.
3. *Response to supply and demand changes (fast/slow)*. The speed of response to changes in supply and demand varies with the level of skill involved. A shortage of highly-skilled chefs cannot be made up quickly simply by raising the pay because it takes time to train people. On the other hand, a shortage of room maids could be made up quickly by a pay adjustment.
4. *Pay level (high/low)*. Markets can vary by level of pay, which is usually determined by level of skill.
5. *Pay distribution (wide/narrow)*. For any given occupation, is the range of pay wide or narrow? It is not difficult to see that if you are looking for someone in a small primary market with a wide distribution of high pay it is a totally different problem from looking for someone in a large secondary market with a narrow distribution of low pay. The strategy will certainly be different.

ECONOMICS OF LABOUR IN HOSPITALITY   103

How, though, can these market characteristics be anticipated from job characteristics? In this respect, there are four key indicators:

1. the level of skill;
2. the degree of specificity (how specific the skills are to an organisation);
3. whether or not performance standard can be measured;
4. the extent to which personal qualities play a part in the job.

The effects of 1 and 2 are fairly obvious – they will change the size of the labour market – but 3 and 4 have an interesting effect. They both represent the possibility of greater individual differences in performance. If standards cannot be formally specified, you are going to get a variety of performances. Similarly, if the jobs require personal characteristics, they are going to get a variety of personal differences. Both have the effect of producing a wider distribution of pay in the market.

To see how jobs can foretell market characteristics, it is helpful to give job characteristics a direction; for example, as shown in Table 11.1. The reverse direction would indicate opposite market characteristics. The model of hotel labour markets (see Chapter 12) suggests that, with the exception of the skilled levels, most hotel and catering recruitment takes place in a market which is secondary in status, large, quick to respond to supply and demand changes and has low pay with wide differentials.

There is an 'active principle' at work in the area where job characteristics meet labour market characteristics – it is a 'substitution effect'. If, for a moment, it is assumed that the larger the labour market the better chance you have of finding what you want cheaply, then it is in the interests of the

Table 11.1 Job characteristics and market type

Job characteristics	Direction	Labour market
Level of skill	The higher	Produces a primary market of small size, slow to react to supply and demand changes, with high pay narrowly distributed
Degree of specificity	The greater	Produces a small market, slow to react to supply and demand change, with high pay narrowly distributed
Measured performance	The greater	Will produce a wider distribution of pay
Personal qualities	The greater	Produces a larger market which responds quickly to supply and demand changes and has a wide distribution of pay

104 THE ECONOMICS OF LABOUR IN HOSPITALITY

employer to design jobs in ways that increase the ability of the organisation to substitute one person for another in the same job. The substitution effect becomes easier ...

- the more unskilled the job;
- the more training is offered by the company;
- the more personal attributes count in the job;
- the less dependent the job is on previous education;
- the more knowledge can be substituted by information;
- the less the degree of specificity.

But, it is not just a question of skill and money.

What has Adam Smith got to say about hospitality jobs?

Quite a lot, but not directly; some old wisdom, however, might to helpful. For Smith, in *Wealth of Nations* it wasn't just earning more money that made a jobseeker choose a particular job; other things entered the equation:

- the agreeableness or disagreeableness of the work, the degree of hardship involved, the honourableness or dishonourableness;
- the easiness or difficulty of learning the job and its attendant cost;
- the degree of security or constancy of the employment;
- the degree of trust and responsibility in the job;
- the probability of success in the job.

According to Smith, all these factors influenced the price of labour because they influenced the decision-maker. Carrying no psychological baggage, these ideas have a timeless common sense about them. Can I learn the job easily? Will I feel comfortable with myself doing the job? Will I be successful? These are questions anyone might ask about becoming a waiter/waitress, a cook, a receptionist, a manager and a porter. Not everyone has a positive attitude to serving other people. Dealing with the general public is never easy; constantly helping others with a smile is not everybody's source of satisfaction. It will be for some, but others might feel uncomfortable in a service role even if all the other attributes could be competently handled. You might not like standing on your feet all day, but standing on soft carpet and not on a hard floor by a machine in a factory may be preferable! It is these nuanced propensities that sidestep money, which Smith is referring too.

The idea of internal labour markets

The notion that hospitality skills can easily be acquired leads us to examine the market implications of that. While the conventional wisdom argues that

ECONOMICS OF LABOUR IN HOSPITALITY **105**

in the external labour market skills are distributed by the price of labour, there may be completely different rules at work within the organisation. These rules are known as the internal labour market.

The concept of the internal labour market is based on the idea that sets of rules and conventions form within organisations which act as allocative mechanisms governing the movement of people and the pricing of jobs. Such rules are about promotion criteria, training opportunities, pay differentials and the evaluation of jobs, but most importantly, they are about which jobs are 'open' to the external labour market. It is the concept of openness which represents the interface between what goes on inside the organisation and the external labour market.

Management have a choice as to what rules they use to govern internal affairs, but should they choose not to use rules, then they open up their organisation to the influence of the external labour market. Like everything else, it is a question of degree. It is possible to envisage two extremes – a strong and a weak internal labour market. Table 11.2 illustrates the dimensions of an internal labour market.

It is important to add that the appellations strong or weak are purely descriptive; there is nothing intrinsically meritorious about 'strong' or pejorative about 'weak'. The question arises as to why managers should direct their policies in a particular direction. The arguments in favour of a strong internal labour market revolve around the benefits of stability.

There are three basic conditions which promote the formation of strong internal labour markets; all are concerned with stability. First, and above all, such markets are likely to form where the technological process decrees that skills in the organisation are very specific to that organisation. The effect of

Table 11.2 Dimension of internal labour markets

Strong	**Weak**
Structural features	*Structural features*
Specified hiring standards	Unspecified hiring standards
Single port of entry	Multiple ports of entry
High skill specificity	Low skill specificity
Continuous on-job training	No on-job training
Fixed criteria for promotion and transfer	No fixed criteria for promotion and transfer
Strong workplace customs	Weak workplace customs
Pay differentials remain fixed over time	Pay differentials vary over time

THE ECONOMICS OF LABOUR IN HOSPITALITY

this is to throw the burden of training on the organisation because, at best, the external labour market can only provide a generalised or approximate capability.

Second, where the type of skill lends itself to being learnt more easily and cheaply by on-the-job training, the burden of training is taken up by existing employees. Hence management will need stability.

Third, where jobs are not easily definable and output not yet open to exact measurement, or where discretion and judgement by employees are unavoidable, then custom and practice with its continuity becomes important. Here again, stability is a desirable state. In these circumstances, in addition to the intrinsic benefits of stability, management also make gains through reduced labour turnover and recruitment costs, together with efficient and cheaper training. For the workforce, there is greater job security, open promotion channels, better training opportunities and pay enhanced by training responsibilities.

Such cosiness could be upset by the external labour market supplying better and cheaper people. Basically, if it could it would. It is only when it simply cannot because the skills needed are so organisation-specific that internal labour markets become dominant.

If all these benefits are going to be realised, then it is essential for a strong internal labour market to keep the external labour market out of the picture. If every job in the organisation is a 'port of entry' – i.e. open to outsiders and there are no hiring criteria, then the organisation is totally 'open' to the outside world. Conversely, if ports of entry are restricted to a few jobs and strict hiring standards applied, then the organisation is fairly 'closed' to the vagaries and caprice of the external labour market.

Once entry is restricted, then allocation of people and skills within the organisation is based on the training capacity of existing resources and on rational progressions strongly related to the technological process. In other words, with restricted and controlled entry, the organisation can build on the job progressions and promotion sequences based on technological and functional priorities, both arranged with suitable incentives. As long as technological priorities remain the same we would expect to find pay differentials remaining fixed over time.

If, on the other hand, an organisation does not need the benefits of a stable workforce, then the merits of a weak internal labour market become apparent. These merits include granting a degree of flexibility of response to fluctuations in demand, a strong emphasis on training the unskilled and the injection of new blood.

If the problem is to assess an organisation on the strong-weak dimension, an obvious clue would be the rate of labour turnover. If internal labour markets are about restricting the power of the external, or about 'locking' employees into a bureaucratic employment relationship, we would expect to find low rates of labour turnover associated with strong internal labour markets and high with weak. This, however, can only be a rough indication. Basically,

ECONOMICS OF LABOUR IN HOSPITALITY **107**

there are five areas of measurability: the specificity of selection criteria; the degree of openness; the extent of on-the-job training; the rate of internal promotions; and the fixity of pay differentials over time. This information could be collected directly using a variety of methods. It is also possible to collect data on management practices in relation to labour, as these are linked to the 'rules' existing in the internal labour market. The rationale for this is that, in theory, management have a complete range of options open to them with respect to the external market, such as being able to:

- alter pay and conditions;
- alter hiring standards;
- alter training policies;
- use overtime and other forms of increased labour supply;
- alter promotion criteria;
- extend ports of entry, redesign jobs.

There are others, but the point here is that choosing to foster a strong labour market may subsequently constrain management's use of these alternative options. In this way, management behaviour at the interface of two labour markets is a good general indicator of the character of the organisation's internal labour market.

Summary

The intention has been to introduce some basic economic ideas about labour markets in order for the reader to understand the anatomy of hotel and catering labour markets, which follows in the next chapter. Notice I have expanded the label 'hospitality' deliberately to introduce parts of industry that share common skills with hospitality. Of particular relevance will be the notion of internal labour markets.

Further reading

Hage, J. (1989) 'The sociology of traditional economic problems: products and labor markets', *Work and Occupations*, 16, 4: 416–445.

Why read this? Though quite old and not about hospitality, this paper offers, by focusing down on the nature of jobs and their consequent labour markets, a way of understanding hospitality in labour economic terms.

CHAPTER

12 Hotel and catering labour markets

In this chapter, the concept of a hospitality industry has been deliberately split into hotels and catering. The rationale for this is that we need to understand the labour market that services them both but also that mobility between these sectors is an important explanation for the levels of pay in both. The purpose here is to paint a portrait of a labour market in such a way as to show how its economic imperatives and technical imperatives are integrated by structures and behavioural patterns.

Chapter objectives

The aim of this chapter is to build a model of the market that incorporates the roles of both skill and mobility. More specifically the objectives are:

- to understand the importance of labour mobility to skill acquisition;
- to understand the importance of labour mobility to pay determination;
- to outline a model of the labour market for hospitality in its widest definition;
- to highlight the special relationship between recruitment and labour turnover.

The mere fact that we can speak of a hotel and catering labour market means that in some way the market has been defined. Usually markets are defined by a set of skills represented by occupations and supplied to particular organisations. In the case of the hotel and catering market, the market itself is fairly conspicuous. You don't have to be in it to recognise certain obvious features, such as:

- a fairly large proportion of unskilled occupations;
- the transferability of skills at any level between a broad range of hotel and catering establishments;
- often, but not invariably, high levels of labour turnover;
- low levels of pay, particularly for unskilled work.

These four features are not unconnected. A large proportion of unskilled or semi-skilled occupations means that these jobs are connected to the general unskilled labour market. Because they can be learnt quickly on the job, such jobs are available to the unskilled workforce. Parts of that unskilled workforce will not be permanently attached to the labour market at all. In other words, hotel and catering recruitment is not just concerned with competing with other firms, it is also a matter of inducing people into the labour market from domestic life.

The fact that a cook can ply their trade in a hotel, a restaurant, a pub, a hospital, a school, an industrial canteen, a ship or anywhere else where a cook might be required, and the fact that such a cook may perform anywhere between the highest and lowest levels of this skill, means that such a person would have a wide range of establishments in which to look for work. In other words, they could transfer their skills widely, but only within the hotel and catering industry. Such a person would have to retrain to enter the building industry, for example. What all this means is that hotel and catering skills are specific to a particular industry and in such circumstances we expect to find mobility mainly *within* the hotel and catering industry, with mobility into and out of the industry confined to unskilled jobs and to questions of attachment to the labour market itself. Broadly speaking, this is what we find.

As pay is deemed to be the market mechanism, analysis of any labour market must focus on explaining the general level of pay. However, in the case of the hotel and catering industry we have a market very clearly determined by a set of skills, therefore the task of describing the market mechanism is mainly one of explaining *how the pay structure and skill structure integrate*. The purpose will be to identify and differentiate the behaviour of the market participants – that is, both employers and workers – and then to explain the measurable activities of the market itself, such as: pay levels, pay differentials, patterns of mobility and market segmentation.

What follows is an attempt to build a model which will meet this requirement. It is founded on the identification of three major influences on the market. These are:

1. the nature of the skills involved – a skill model;
2. the constantly fluctuating nature of consumer demand;
3. the existence of market segmentation, founded upon social and unsocial hours of work.

The nature of the skills involved – a skill model

The construction of a skill model is in three stages, each with its attendant problems. The first stage is actually to describe and differentiate skills. The problems here are:

*   hotels employ a large range of occupations and skills;

THE ECONOMICS OF LABOUR IN HOSPITALITY

- occupational titles only describe a type of skill, not a level of skill. The term 'cook' conveys only an activity;
- skill levels overlap other sectors of the industry;
- the problem of drawing a line between what is skilled and unskilled.

The first task is to unhinge the concept of skill from the mask of occupation. A simple rough classification is helpful here.

1. Managerial.
2. Supervisory.
3. Craft.
4. Operative.

Accepting that managing and supervising are skilled activities, the difficulty comes in separating craft from operative. Qualifications help us to define craft. Thus, vocational qualifications in cooking, service waiting, wine waiting, accounting and reception determined the craft category. The distinction that craft equals skilled and that operative means semi-skilled and unskilled is plausible in this context. The distinction between skilled and unskilled is that skill requires some form of formal training or education and cannot be solely learnt by on-the-job training. Consequently, unskilled implies that work can be learnt solely on the job.

The next task is to estimate the proportion of skilled to unskilled per establishment. There are two issues here; are there occupations that vary in skill level by the type of establishment and does the proportion of skilled to unskilled vary?

The place to start here is with the occupational structure of establishments. Table 12.1 is an example of three major types of establishment and their occupational structure. There are, of course, other sectors of the industry, but these are always present and are always large sectors.

In respect of the first question, is it possible to pick out which occupations might vary in skill status by type of establishment? Some reasonable assumptions are necessary here.

If we assume that managers and supervisors are skilled, what of the others? The candidates for the category 'sometimes skilled' are chefs and waiters.

Table 12.1 The occupational structure of hospitality establishments

	Hotel %	Restaurant %	Industrial catering %
Management	5	15	7
Supervisory	9	6	8
Craft	20	27	17
Operative	66	52	68

It would depend on the class of establishment. Receptionists are more likely to be skilled, irrespective of the class of establishment. The rest could be allocated to the unskilled or semi-skilled category, which equates in our classification to operative. Accepting that there must be exceptions, the guiding principle for the skill model is that the occupations which can vary between operative and craft classifications are chefs and waiter/waitress.

The question which is yet unresolved is – do the proportions vary with size of unit? Again, some reasonable assumptions are necessary here. There is a prima facie case for saying that the skill proportions don't change with size. Surely as hotels get bigger they need more unskilled maids, but larger hotels tend to have more function rooms and higher levels of service, creating more chefs, and everyone knows more elaborate cooking means more washing up! In this way, skill breeds unskilled work. It would not be taking too much licence to say that the skill proportions are linear and – like a nest of Russian dolls – they are the same whatever the size. This is an assumption of our model and is illustrated in Figure 12.1.

What the proportion triangle doesn't capture is that there must be graduations of skill within the skill category. The third stage, therefore, is to conceive the industry as a hierarchy of units with the same skill proportions but with the absolute value of skill rising as the hierarchy ascends.

While it is perfectly legitimate to analyse the industry by its component sections, such as hotels, restaurants, industrial catering, hospitals etc., what has to be realised is that each of these contains a hierarchy of standards representing a range of customer or contract spending. To simplify matters, the industry can be visualised in two broad components – on the one hand, hotels and restaurants; and on the other, all forms of institutional catering. This division emphasises different forms of commercial trading but – perhaps more

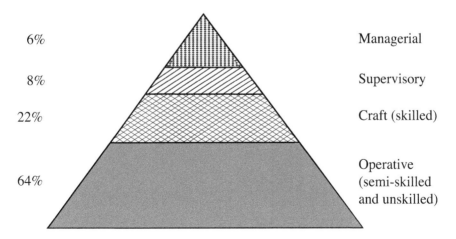

Figure 12.1 Skill structure of hospitality units

THE ECONOMICS OF LABOUR IN HOSPITALITY

important to the market – different demands on labour in terms of working hours. Figure 12.2 represents the industry skill structure. The pyramid for the hotel and restaurant sector is taller than for the institutional sector on the assumption that the higher end of the price range demands the highest standard of skills.

This model assumes that the mobility pattern is in three streams; unskilled entrance at all levels; skill is accumulated by mobility up the pyramids; and movement of skilled labour from hotels and restaurants to institutional catering. This mobility pattern is founded on certain crucial assumptions about the capacity of units to train. In terms of capacity of any one establishment, we assume that:

- every establishment has an *upper limit to its capacity to teach*. Standards are for guests not staff, and they do not change overnight. Any movement upwards tends to be gradual. Once the skills have been mastered, further acquisition must be through moving to an establishment with higher standards;

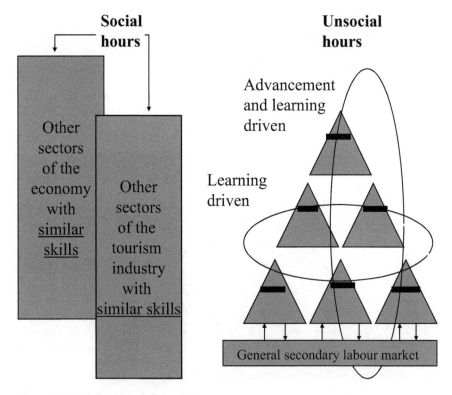

Figure 12.2 Skill and mobility model

HOTEL AND CATERING LABOUR MARKETS   113

- although skills are transferable, there are barriers within the establishment to changing occupations. A waiter cannot simply change to a receptionist; a receptionist cannot become a cook etc. This *occupational rigidity* is not solely confined to the skilled occupations;
- every establishment has a capacity to undertake on-the-job training and formal training to cope with the influx of unskilled and semi-skilled people.

It has also been assumed that there exists two labour markets segmented into one which works the same hours as the general population and one which works different hours. These are termed social and unsocial hours markets. This is subject to cultural variations, but what is important here is that if it is assumed that both markets offer the same pay and are in other respects the same, one has an advantage in hours. If Figure 12.2 is correct, people can transfer from hotels and restaurants to institutional catering without loss of material benefit, depending on the pay differentials between the two sectors. Given the circumstances of a hierarchy of establishments and an alternative market with social hours, it follows that:

- individuals in the craft, supervisory and managerial categories seeking to learn will use the hierarchy of establishments to acquire more and higher skills;
- skilled individuals will sometimes work at levels below their skill capacity.

The contribution of the skill model is that it puts forward enabling conditions which create pressures to be mobile, such as:

1. the transferability of skills across all sectors of the industry;
2. the non-transferability of skills across occupational boundaries;
3. the 'skill pyramid' structure of the industry offering mobility as a means of skill acquisition;
4. on-the-job training capacity;
5. the existence of a top limit to the capacity for skill and knowledge learning in each unit;
6. the opportunity to work at below the maximum skill level without loss of material benefit.

Thus, mobility offers a means for both the individual wishing to acquire skills and the individual looking to use less of their skills.

So far, the emphasis has been on the skilled, but before we conclude the skill model, some discussion is required on the nature of the unskilled work. It is one thing to say that as the unskilled proportion is the greater the industry will always have a surplus supply because it is connected to the general unskilled labour market and can quickly train people, but it is quite another

THE ECONOMICS OF LABOUR IN HOSPITALITY

to actually recruit in that large market. Three aspects of hotel and catering unskilled work are important here.

1. Unskilled jobs are not machine minding; they are a bundle of low-level tasks which, no matter how menial, require a degree of self-organisation.
2. The effort and character of individuals actually counts in performance, therefore there will be individual differences in performance.
3. Productivity does not depend on job tenure to any large degree.

The skill model and pay

The influence of the skill model on pay is as follows:

* the higher proportion of unskilled jobs tends to create a surplus supply which depresses rates of pay;
* competition is encouraged by the hierarchical skill structure and by the fact that individual attributes actually count;
* the skill structure encourages mobility;
* as productivity does not depend on job tenure, there is little incentive to reward long service;
* the existence of alternative markets, with different hours of work, allows workers to trade off skill and hours.

By far the most important of these influences is the encouragement of a surplus of supply by the unskilled nature of the work. This has significance for both managerial and market behaviour. If the surplus keeps pay down, then it is *always in the interests of managers to de-skill*. If there is always a surplus, then supply will be elastic – that is, responsive to small changes in the price of labour.

Let's hear it for high pay!

What the model is good at is making clear that the labour market itself is a source of learning and that deflationary pressures are ever present in the structure of the market. What it is not so good at is showing how pay can be high. The inflationary pressures are not so conspicuous, but competition is competition, particularly for skilled and managerial talent. One notable characteristic of hospitality is that occupations that carry the same label are differentially valued in different organisations. From the outside this is difficult to appreciate because the same job title carries numerous differences in detail. Nevertheless, there are many well paid jobs in the industry – in the managerial and skilled occupations – particularly when jobs overlap with the generic business labour market. Hospitality management is a very skilled occupation requiring a range of personal attributes that are not easily located in the generic market. It is this specialised knowledge that leads to higher pay.

HOTEL AND CATERING LABOUR MARKETS **115**

In one sense the model is incomplete in that although it is built upon the ease in which skills can be learnt this very fact leads to higher earning through the root of entrepreneurship.Compared with many industries, setting up a business in hospitality is relatively simple, and the technical skills involved can be quickly acquired. Entrepreneurship is one of the highest paid categories in the industry, and many people leave the model to go in that direction.

Is recruitment related to labour turnover?

If, as implied by the model, there is so much mobility inherent in the hotel and catering labour market, then how does that affect the recruitment function? There is an interesting and important message here; one aspect of labour market behaviour that is universal enough to be predictable – so reliable in fact that it should enter all calculations of recruitment. What is this potent factor? Quite simply, it is the common sense notion that 'the longer a person stays in a job, the less likely they are to leave'. In reverse this reads: 'a person is more likely to leave a job the shorter their period of service in that job'. The uncertainties of a job and surroundings are likely to be greater when a person first enters a job – does it meet expectations? It is in this early period that a person has a high propensity to leave. Conversely, the longer a person stays in a job the more comfortable it becomes; it begins to fit like an old overcoat.

This behavioural tendency has real significance for labour management because it unites recruitment with labour turnover. The golden rule is that the rate of each rises and falls together with just a short time lag. When recruitment goes up, so does labour turnover. This may astound. Surely when business is expanding people will want to stay? Maybe, but when business is expanding and therefore has an abnormal number of new recruits with a high propensity to leave, then labour turnover is higher than normal.

An example case of expansion

Suppose a company needs to substantially increase its manpower in respect of one particular occupation. For years it has employed sixty people, and 20 per cent leave every year. Half of these vacancies are filled by promotion from a lower grade, and the rest are made up by recruitment from the external labour market. The situation would be:

Existing staff	Labour turnover	Promotion	Recruitment
60	12	6	?

Let's leave the recruitment figure blank for a moment. If the company needed to expand, say, to ninety, then the question of recruitment and a recruitment budget becomes crucial. An obvious projection of what might be needed would be:

Existing staff	Labour turnover	Promotion	Recruitment	Target
60	12	6	36	90

But it would be wrong because it assumes that the labour turnover percentage will remain at 20 per cent when it will not. Expansion means recruiting more newcomers with a higher than normal propensity to leave. In reality, the company will have to recruit more than the thirty-six projected in order to achieve the target of ninety. The real situation might progress differently:

Existing staff	Labour turnover	Promotion	Recruitment	Target
60	25	6	49	90

The recruitment budget would need to be larger to be more realistic. To repeat, as recruitment rises so does labour turnover. It is equally important in a period of contraction, where cutting staff numbers by stopping recruitment is a flawed policy.

Summary

In this chapter we have described a model of how the hotel and catering labour market actually works. It is a dynamic model which is driven by skill differentials which in turn emanate from class differentials in the consumer market. It highlights the influence of both mobility and structure on pay and invites those interested in working and building a career in hospitality to see the market as a learning experience.

Further reading

Riley, M. and Szivas, E. (2003) 'Pay determination: a socio-economic framework', *Annals of Tourism Research*, 30, 2: 446–464.

Why read this? Management are free agents to set rates of pay, but this paper outlines in detail the inflationary and deflationary pressures within the economic sphere of tourism and hospitality that influence management decisions on pay. The same arguments are laid out explicitly in: Riley, M., Ladkin, A. and Szivas, E. (2002) *Tourism Employment: Analysis and Planning*, Clevedon: Channel View Publications, ch. 4.

CHAPTER

13 Throughput management – productivity

To be clear from the start, the problem for productivity in hospitality is that consumer demand is always variable and that customers select from the services and products offered, which invariably leaves some unused. Productivity management is therefore about adaptability to this uncertainty – it is a response issue. It is easy to say but not so easy to do. In hospitality, for the rational efficiency advocates, the awkward issue is always that of quality and more specifically defining quality in a way that fits measurement.

Chapter objectives

- to explain the concept of productivity as it applies to hospitality;
- to differentiate actual productivity from measures of it;
- to illustrate how labour supply can be matched to consumer demand;
- to introduce and to evaluate functional flexibility.

The hospitality context

One way of defining quality is to throw bodies at it! The more uniformed servers there are the higher the quality of service. This is a crude assessment but not too far from the truth. Can it really be possible to apply the rational efficiency of a hamburger chain to all hospitality establishments? The arguments on organisations in Chapter 10 suggest not. You might think that services are immune from such rational thinking, but the industry is more rational and clinical than customers observe. Cleaning rooms and supplying dishes can be run on industrial lines and often are. The real problem lies with the concept of quality; how do managers define it and more importantly how do customers see it. A concern for quality does not deny the case for rational efficiency, but it makes it hard to sustain.

It is an economic issue

The initial feasibility of most hospitality operations is built around estimated capital and throughput applied in an input/output calculation, but when up

THE ECONOMICS OF LABOUR IN HOSPITALITY

and running it is actual throughput that becomes vital to success. It is often said that the customer is king, but in the sphere of productivity where value is created, the throughput of customers is always king. In Chapter 11 it was pointed out that one of the building blocks of hospitality economics was the rate and variation of consumer demand. In this chapter we talk about managing that variation. This means we are concerned with productivity. The purpose is to draw attention to the fundamentals of productivity and present a simple descriptive framework which displays the factors which contribute to productivity in hospitality. The concern throughout is with actual productivity, not with relative productivity, nor with the measures used to make comparisons. At the outset it is important to note that productivity is different from profitability and that ownership is irrelevant to the case for productivity and therefore considerations of such modern trends as out-sourcing are not an issue. Whoever is responsible needs to be productive.

Conceptualising productivity

Productivity is always difficult to understand because it is hard to separate the concept from its close cousin profitability; a problem made even harder by the issue of delineating measures of productivity from the process that actually produced it. The hospitality industry shares these problems. In the first case it is often, and not unreasonably, subsumed under concerns for profitability. And, in the second, there is confusion between how it is measured and how it is produced. There is a problem of poor joinery between notions of what productivity is and how it might be measured. In other words, measurement does not always capture exactly how a level of productivity was achieved. Something has to be enacted to produce productivity, and common measurement such as by comparisons does not capture this.

It is not at all uncommon to find some very sophisticated arguments surrounding the concept of productivity – what it is and how it should be measured can get very complicated sometimes. Economics, for example, uses input/output models to determine productivity, whereby the level of input causes the output and expresses results as, what they call, a production function. Whilst this approach is indisputably correct, it is at the same time problematic for hospitality, where productivity is driven not by inputs but by the output side – that is, variations in demand – it is the reverse of the standard production function. Hotels and food service operations of any kind are part of a class of units which share characteristics of having perishable products, a within unit product range and a demand which is variable in the very short term. To complicate the problem further, hoteliers concerned for profitability, quite rightly, are more likely to focus on the many metrics, such as RevPAR, that are revenue and market based. The performance of revenue management and marketing prowess are essential and must be to the fore in management's thinking. However, if they look the other way they will see cost and need for control, which come together in the idea of productivity, which is about

THROUGHPUT MANAGEMENT – PRODUCTIVITY **119**

optimally deploying resources. Although it can be indicated by measures, the outcomes of any level of productivity work their way through in normal business measures such as profitability. In the same way as intelligence tests provide indicators of intelligence but do not measure it, productivity measures only capture indicators of it and not of how it is produced.

Labour productivity

For labour economic and HRM, the issue of how to measure productivity is secondary to producing it. How it is produced in hospitality is by managing variable costs; the principal one being labour. Labour is an input that needs to be matched to output (in the case of hospitality – consumer demand). It is important to be clear at the outset what the major assumption is – namely, that in terms of an input/output model, hotels and catering operations exhibit the reverse of the normal economic assumption that inputs determine output. Here it is being suggested that output, which is inconsistent and uncertain, drives input. In truth, both these ideas on productivity are true and compatible, but they exist at different levels. The demand-driven model is at the operational level, while the input/output model is a macro level overall measure of business performance.

The essential problem

Hospitality operations have a demand which is variable in the very short run. This characteristic bequeaths to the task of achieving and measuring productivity two intractable problems, which are:

- that of having to account for very short-term changes in demand;
- (because there is a range of services and products) having to account for the discrepancy between those consumed and those provided but not consumed.

These problems can be most usefully seen as two sources of uncertainty: never being sure how many customers will arrive, and not knowing what they will consume from what is on offer. Offering a wide range may be an enticement to customers, but if they chose narrowly there is a productivity problem. Reconciling this conundrum is at the heart of productivity and successful hospitality management.

Responding to the problem

At least in the conceptual sense, labour-intensive service industries have it rather easy for the simple reason that the demand for labour is direct. Labour does not have to depend on the productivity of a machine. Instead, labour is demanded for what it can produce directly – clean a room, serve a

THE ECONOMICS OF LABOUR IN HOSPITALITY

drink, escort a tour etc. There are two very important implications of this, which are:

1. that productivity is essentially about physical productivity and human capacity with all the scope for variation that that implies;
2. that the origin of demand for labour is sales. A pattern of sales or forecast pattern of sales is simultaneously a pattern of demand for labour.

It follows from this that productivity in labour-intensive service industries is essentially about the utilisation of labour, and in this respect there are two essential management tasks, which are:

1. to manage the physical output by designing jobs in such a way as to ensure efficient working practices and best technological methods, while at the same time setting a hiring standard in terms of personal capacity to suit the job;
2. to manage the relationship between a forecast demand for labour and the actual supply of labour. Above all else, productivity is about efficiently matching labour supply to demand.

The two tasks share different problems but one solution. On the one hand, how is physical efficiency or personal capacity on the job to be defined and judged? On the other hand, how is a sales forecast to be translated into a forecast demand for labour? In fact, the solution to the first question becomes the solution to the second as well and that is if a set of performance standards are applied. A performance standard is an expression of output measured by a time period; for example, if the unit of time is the man-day, then the performance standard for room cleaners might be sixteen rooms per man-day or for cooks 120 covers per man-day.

Setting a performance standard

Two things need to be said about setting performance standards straight away. First, for every occupation they are personal to a particular operation and therefore not transferable between operations; and second, they are easier to set for some jobs than others. That said, the setting of a performance standard requires a full work study analysis using all appropriate techniques. The tests and timings must be done on the basis that:

- the best possible methods are being used;
- all possible technological substitutions have taken place;
- the final timings are based not on the best or the worst or the average workers but on an above average worker who represents a standard that can be sustained by the training and supervision functions.

THROUGHPUT MANAGEMENT – PRODUCTIVITY **121**

The choice of measuring unit and time span should be appropriate to the job in question. For room cleaners, the choice is obvious – the number of rooms cleaned, as is the number of journeys for a room service waiter and the number of covers for a regular waiter. The choice of time period depends on the problem you suspect you have. If you suspect a part of the workforce is at times overstretched and at other times underused, use a unit which splits these periods; for example, journeys per hour might well reveal large variations through the day of a room service department.

A performance standard has four direct functions:

1. it allows a sales forecast to be translated into a demand for labour;
2. it provides a guide to the hiring standard;
3. it is an objective for the training function;
4. it allows actual productivity to be compared with forecast productivity.

It is worth making the point that it is not necessary to measure the productivity of every job, but it is important to do so where numbers employed vary directly with the level of business.

Translating sales into a demand forecast for labour

Once a performance standard is in place, its key function is to allow management to translate a sales forecast into a forecast demand for labour. This function is crucial to productivity. To illustrate just how crucial it is, it is appropriate to return to that central characteristic of life in the hotel and catering industry – short-term sales instability.

Figure 13.1 shows two identical patterns of variation and one that strays. Line SF is a forecast of sales on a daily basis and shows enormous variations from day to day.

If the demand for labour is direct, then a line representing the labour demand LD would exactly shadow line SF. Now, in a perfect world the actual supply of labour (LS) would follow the pattern of the other two lines exactly. Alas, we don't live in a perfect world, and the actual productivity task of management is to make labour supply match labour demand. It is not an exact science, because the starting point is a sales forecast which could be wrong, but you have to work from something. Having a performance standard allows the manager to translate line SF into line LD.

In conditions of fluctuating business, the manager has two objectives, which are:

- to regulate labour supply to match demand;
- to determine the proportion of fixed labour supply to variable labour supply.

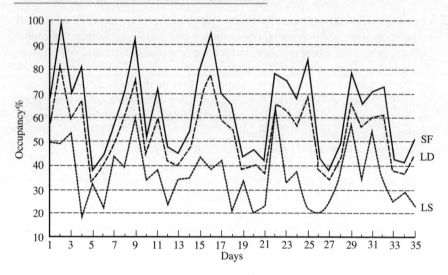

Figure 13.1 A short-term forecast of demand and labour supply

To achieve these objectives requires a seven stage process in which an estimate of labour supply should enable managers to adjust supply to meet the forecast targets.

1. Determine a system of forecasting demand (sales forecast) – operations should have a sales forecast for several reasons besides workload analysis. However, for whatever reason a forecast exists, the frequency of the forecast – i.e. monthly, weekly, daily or hourly – will depend to an extent on how much scope management actually have to adjust labour supply. If you can only adjust monthly, then it is pointless measuring the workload daily!
2. The classification of the job – the jobs which really require analysis are those which 'vary directly with the level of business'. However, in practice it is not so easy to classify jobs into direct 'sales related' and 'non-related' – there are many grey areas.
3. Determine an appropriate unit of measure for each direct job.
4. Turn the unit of measure into a performance standard. For example:

Job group	Performance standard	Time unit (hours)
Waiter/waitress	20 covers	4
Cooks	90 covers	8
Room cleaners	15 rooms	8
Bar staff	$400	8

THROUGHPUT MANAGEMENT – PRODUCTIVITY **123**

5. Translate the sales forecast into a forecast for the demand for labour by using the performance standards.
6. Compare forecast labour demand with forecast labour supply.
7. Adjust.

An example for room cleaners:

Sales forecast	390 rooms
Performance standard	15 per man-day
Demand for labour	26 man-days (390 ÷ 15)
Estimated labour supply	24 man-days
Adjustment	+ 2 man-days

It is worth emphasising that as the process works from a forecast and ends with some kind of adjustment to labour supply, the possibility exists that the forecast may not match what actually happens. So it is not an exact science, and adjustments may over- or under-compensate. It is also worth stating that this process is available on software in which the unique input from the user is the performance standard.

Earlier, it was stated that there were two objectives in the task of utilising labour efficiently in conditions of fluctuating demand. The following examples show how these two objectives are addressed by the technique.

Objective 1 – matching labour supply and demand

Table 13.1 is an example of a workload analysis for a seven-day forecast of room sales for a hotel. The occupation under measurement is room maid and there are thirty-two maids employed.

Column 1 = Daily estimate of room sales produced by rolling forecast technique; Column 2 = Performance standard; Column 3 = Man-day requirement or

Table 13.1 Forecast and workload prediction

1 Room sales	2 PS	3 Requirement	4 FT staff	5 Staff dist	6 Room dist
375	15	25	23	–2	–30
420	15	28	23	–5	–75
480	15	32	23	–9	–135
210	15	14	23	+9	+135
480	15	32	23	–9	–135
360	15	24	23	–1	–15
300	15	20	23	+3	+45

THE ECONOMICS OF LABOUR IN HOSPITALITY

demand for labour (Column 1 ÷ Column 2); Column 4 = Number of full-time staff on duty or estimated labour supply. The estimate of labour supply should be expressed in terms of numbers on duty, which will differ from total numbers employed – to get the figure, total number employed should be adjusted to their actual daily hours; e.g. if a room cleaner works a five day, forty hour week and you employ thirty-two room cleaners, the daily supply of labour is:

$32 \times 40 = 1280$ total LS per week
to get total LS per day $\div 7 \times 5 = 914$ hours/day
to get the LS per day $\div 40 = 23$ room cleaners

Column 5 = Difference between requirement (Column 3) and estimated labour supply (Column 4). A minus means a shortage and a plus means an excess; Column 6 = The differences in Column 5 are expressed as room differences simply by multiplying Column 5 by Column 2. This column can be seen as representing under- or overcapacity.

The purpose of Table 13.1 is to show the manager where oversupply or undersupply will occur. In this example, on five days there is a projected shortage, and on two of those days it is sizeable. The argument is that the situation is manageable in advance once the position is clear.

Objective 2 – estimating the optimum level of full-time employment

There is no exact way of measuring the optimum level of full-time employment, but the same productivity analysis that helps to match supply with demand also offers a trial and error solution. The principle is: given any forecast of sales, what estimate of mismatch is produced by every possible range of full-time employment. Table 13.2 uses the same room forecast as Table 13.1,

Table 13.2 Estimating employment level from a forecast

Room forecast	Employment level								
	28	29	30	31	32	33	34	35	36
375	−75	−60	−52	−45	−30	−22	−15	−	+15
420	−120	−105	−97	−90	−75	−67	−60	−45	−30
480	−180	−165	−157	−150	−135	−127	−120	−105	−90
210	+90	+105	+112	+120	+135	+142	+150	+165	+180
480	−180	−165	−157	−150	−135	−127	−120	−105	−90
360	−60	−45	−37	−30	−15	−7	−	+15	+30
300	−	+15	+22	+30	+45	+52	+60	+75	+90

THROUGHPUT MANAGEMENT – PRODUCTIVITY **125**

but this time the room difference calculation is carried out for a range of employment levels from twenty-eight to thirty-six.

Clearly, how these figures are interpreted will depend on the ease or difficulty the hotel has in adjusting labour supply. Here, 34–35 looks manageable.

What has to be emphasised is that because the problem is fluctuations in business the measurement technique is by necessity 'trial and error' and strongly dependent on the conditions of adjustment.

The comparison of actual productivity with forecast productivity

In addition to being an aid to forecasting, the performance standard also allows management to reverse the process and ask: 'how productive were we?' After all the forecasting and adjusting has been done, an actual amount of business occurs in a particular period and it is then possible to use the performance standard to examine exactly what did happen: how accurate was the forecast? How accurate was the adjustment? The example shown in Table 13.3 simplifies the process by using only room sales on one day.

In this simple example the hotel was overstaffed, which produced an actual performance standard of 13.6 rooms per room cleaner (actual sales divided by actual supply) instead of the standard 15.

This concept of using the performance standard to analyse actual business brings labour management directly into the budgeting and accounting systems. The figure for actual labour supply can always be obtained through timesheets or wage documentation. This means that once broken down by appropriate activities the various performance standards can be used to compare the performance of these activities in different periods in the past.

Managing labour supply – contingent techniques

The key to efficient labour utility is not the measurement of productivity but the flexibility of labour supply which follows from that measurement. It is through the actual adjustment that productivity is achieved. The extent to which management can adjust is very much subject to prevailing conditions

Table 13.3 Labour supply adjustment

Forecast sales 390 rooms	Actual sales 360 rooms
• Performance standard 15	• Performance standard 15
Forecast demand 26 man-days for labour	Actual demand 24 man-days for labour
Forecast labour 24 man-days supply	Actual supply 26.5 man-days
Adjustment +2 man-days	Surplus/deficit +2.5 man-days Actual 13.6 rooms productivity

THE ECONOMICS OF LABOUR IN HOSPITALITY

Table 13.4 Option for supply adjustment

Reduce demand	Adjustment mechanism for labour supply
Reduce services	Increase personal productivity
Substitute technology	Recruitment
	Labour turnover
	Absenteeism
	Overtime
	Staff adjustment
	Shift realignment
	Flexible hours
	Increase part-time work
	Casualisation
	Days off
	Holidays
	Contract work
	Increase internal mobility
	Retirement
	Redundancy
	Natural wastage
	Lay off
	Pay

in both the external and internal labour markets and, where applicable, the conditions of the union agreement. That said, a range of options given to management is as shown in Table 13.4.

On a day-to-day basis, not all these options are open; technological substitution, for example, requires considerable planning. Given the short time span in which adjustments have to be made, the most common methods of extending labour supply are: overtime, some form of bonus system, casual labour and part-time employment. At the very least, management should be aware of, and have compared, the cost of these alternatives. Again it is important to state that subcontracting simply transfers this same process to another organisation.

Always the bridesmaid: productivity and functional flexibility

Functional flexibility seems on paper to be a practical approach to contingent manipulation of labour resources in an ever-changing context, but it

THROUGHPUT MANAGEMENT – PRODUCTIVITY   127

never seems to arrive. This approach advocates functional flexibility, with its implication of training, multi-skilling programmes and a strong internal labour market. It advocates that employees move from job to job internally as required by demand. It is difficult to implement mainly because it has not yet proved itself to have any economic advantage over normal contingent approaches. It would be fairer to say that it is a good idea without, as yet, sufficient economic underpinning. Common sense suggests that total substitutability – that is, everyone able to do everyone else's job – is unobtainable and probably undesirable as well, but how much flexibility is actually needed and is there an optimal? It is a question of the cross-utilisation of labour under conditions of variable demand but with fixed parameters (maximum capacity of the unit).

If we assume a situation in which a unit workforce contains a number of jobs with different skills attached to them and that consumer demand is variable in the short run (i.e. hour, day), then if there is no substitutability, the size of the workforce must equal the highest level of forecast demand for each job that occurs in the period. In these circumstances the residual minimum and the very maximum would be the same! But if 100 per cent substitutability were the case, then the residual minimum would be equal to the highest combined forecast demand across all jobs. Table 13.5 is an example of the principle and describes a hypothetical unit with two jobs over a five-day period in which demand fluctuates. Two further assumptions apply here: first, that the solution must be by internal resources and, second, that transfer of staff between the days is ignored in the five-day planning period.

With no substitutability the minimum workforce size is 28 + 10 = 38. With 100 per cent substitutability it becomes 28 + 6 = 34 a saving of over 10 per cent. The minimum employment levels for each job, given substitutability, can be estimated from the maximum total demand and the maximum demand for the alternative job. Thus, for Job A, the lower parameter would be 34–10 = 24 and for Job B it would be 34–28 = 6. In this example, therefore, it follows that the optimum level of employment for Job A is between 28–24 and for Job B is between 10–6. The optimum combination of A and B is within these parameters. The pairing 28–10 seems excessive, as does the minimum pairing of 24–6 fails on day 4, so the answer is somewhere between.

However, it will not have escaped your notice that at 34 we still have excess labour on four out of the five days. This is because we have made the assumption that all demand will be met at the required level of quality. We have now

Table 13.5 An example of cross-substitutability of labour

Day	1	2	3	4	5
Job/skill A	12	20	17	28	22
Job/skill B	7	10	7	6	5

THE ECONOMICS OF LABOUR IN HOSPITALITY

come to the juncture where notions of productivity actually meet ideas about quality. If we assume that not having enough staff to meet demand adversely affects quality and we wish to maintain quality, then logically we will have to staff up to the highest level of demand. What this example is designed to show is that in some cases the decision to meet all demand creates excess supply even when you have total flexibility. This juncture, where productivity meets quality, is also where the internal approach has to face up to the inevitable need for the external one. The sub-text here is either to accept fluctuating quality or accept fluctuating profits, or to consciously decide not to meet all demand through internal resources. In other words, in constantly fluctuating circumstances, a degree of external manipulation is essential.

Summary

What this chapter has been about is responsiveness; adjusting labour supply to demand. Any resource, not just labour, can be regarded as responsive if it meets any or any combination of the following criteria:

- the degree to which it is more sustainable and less perishable (able to be stored);
- the degree to which it has more than one purpose (flexible utility);
- the degree to which it only incurs costs if used (e.g. casual labour);
- the degree to which it is substitutable (cooking skills for the equivalent bought-in prepared food and vice versa).

Judging a resource by its responsiveness, as distinct from its cost, focuses attention on the performance of the resource, but this is not implying that costs are secondary to efficiency nor that cost considerations are not a full part of valuing a resource.

One business question that is rarely asked is: 'on what does any level of profitability depend?' The obvious answer is sales volume, prices and costs, but whilst this is true, it is not the complete story. All three factors, but particularly costs, are dependent on the productivity of the operation – its efficiency. What this chapter makes clear is, firstly, that efficient control of labour supply is dependent on having a good forecasting procedure for consumer demand and, secondly, that the design of jobs is always worthy of managerial attention. Large-scale establishments have the advantage of computerised forecasting but often lack the ability to multi-skill staff, whilst small establishments tend to adjust labour supply organically as part of everyday life.

Further reading

Riley, M., Ladkin, A. and Szivas, E. (2002) *Tourism Employment: Analysis and Planning*, Clevedon: Channel View Publications, ch. 3.

Why read this? This chapter outlines the broad fundamentals of productivity in hospitality and outlines some managerial strategies. In a similar way to the chapter you have just read, this piece wrestles with the innate difficulties in grasping the concepts for an industry that has unpredictable short-term demand.

Park, S., Yaduma, N., Lockwood, A. and Williams, A. (2016) 'Demand fluctuations, labour flexibility and productivity', *Annals of Tourism Research*, 59: 93–112.

Why read this? Here is some valuable evidence on what is blindingly obvious to industry insiders but rarely acknowledged by the conventional wisdom of economics – that is, that it is the response of labour utilisation to fluctuations in customer demand that determines overall productivity.

The awkward practical problem of trying to measure hospitality productivity in terms of conventional approaches is attacked by the following: Baker, M. and Riley, M. (1994) 'New perspectives on hotel productivity', *International Journal of Hospitality Management*, 13, 4: 7–15.

Why read this? This illustrates just how difficult it is to map hospitality productivity measures on normal economic metrics.

The issue of how quality intervenes in service productivity has a large literature which features defining levels of service and inputting concepts of service into economic models. A good place to start is: Gronroos, C. and Ojasalo, K. (2004) 'Service productivity: towards a conceptualization of the transformation of inputs into economic results in services', *Journal of Business Research*, 57: 414–423.

Why read this? This is a complex paper which focuses on the interpretation of inputs of service into economic approaches to productivity. It leads into a vast literature on service quality.

CHAPTER

14 The measurement of labour turnover and stability

Given that labour mobility is a conspicuous feature of hospitality, the question of measurement needs to be addressed. However, it is also a feature of hospitality establishments that they have a core set of staff who remain. What this implies is that units are both stable and unstable at the same time. This is why the measurement of labour turnover and stability is a useful managerial tool.

Chapter objectives

* to show a simple method calculating labour turnover;
* to show a simple method calculating labour stability.

There are four principal reasons for measurement

1. As explained in Chapter 12, labour turnover determines the rate of recruitment.
2. It is an indication of the state of the external labour market.
3. High instances of labour turnover are usually seen as being bad for the organisation, although skill accumulation does require a degree of mobility.
4. If a rate is measured, then performance can be compared between defined categories such as organisations, individual units, departments, occupations, age groups etc.

The commonest way of measuring labour turnover is the straightforward percentage. The calculation is:

$$\frac{\text{Number of leavers in a specific period}}{\text{Average number of employees during the period}} \times 100$$

The average number of employees during a period is simply calculated by taking the number employed at the beginning of the period and the number at the end of the period and finding the average, for example:

Number of leavers during the year	200
Total number of employed at the beginning of year	400
Total number employed at the end of the year	430

$$\frac{200}{415} \times 100 = 48 \text{ per cent}$$

The merits of this measure are obvious, particularly in comparisons. The rate of labour turnover in different departments or in different establishments can be compared. There are, however, two important drawbacks.

1. If one of the pairs in a comparison has, during the period, undergone a major change in employment level (up or down), then you are not comparing like with like, because the percentage figure doesn't capture the essential relationship between recruitment and labour turnover described in Chapter 17. When reviewing a set of percentages, this *possibility* must be borne in mind. It would be wrong, for example, to compare a unit that had just opened with ones that have been running for some time, on the basis of this measurement.
2. The percentage figure of labour turnover can hide areas of stability within the target population. A figure of 100 per cent labour turnover may be produced by the 400 per cent turnover of a quarter of the target population, thus hiding both a more serious problem and an important characteristic of the majority.

Stability index

If there are many reasons for labour turnover there is one very sound reason for having a measure of stability, and that is that such a measure would be a good indication of the effects of policy change on the conditions in the external labour market. What stability means is the capacity for a firm to retain its labour force. In order for a measure to be useful, it must express this capacity over time and allow for comparisons in the same way as the labour turnover percentage. The stability index fits these conditions well.

This index simply expresses the total length of service of all *present* employees in the time frame as a proportion of the maximum possible stability. This notion of the maximum possible stability simply means: the total length of service if nobody left in the time frame. For example, if a firm employing ten workers was ten years old and everyone who started ten years ago was still with the firm, then the maximum possible stability would be 100 years. If, as in this example, the length of service of present employees is also 100 years, the stability index = 1, which is maximum stability. The stability index goes from 0.0 to 1 and can be turned into a percentage by multiplying by 100. Two examples would be useful.

132 THE ECONOMICS OF LABOUR IN HOSPITALITY

Example 1

A hotel employs 400 people. Let us say that 200 employees have one year's service, 100 have two years' service, fifty have four years' service and fifty have five years' service. The total length of service of all present employees is 850 years.

The period under measurement is five years. The maximum stability is, therefore, 400×5 years = 2000 years.

Stability index =

$$\frac{850}{2000} = 0.42 \text{ or } 42 \text{ per cent}$$

In normal usage, the stability measure looks backwards over time, and often the size of the firm will have changed over time. This is purely a technical problem for the index, and it is resolved as shown in Example 2.

Example 2

As in Example 1, we take a hotel with 400 employees who have a combined length of service of 850 years, only this time the size of the workforce has fluctuated.

Size of workforce 2 years $\times$ 400 = 800
2 years $\times$ 450 = 900
1 year $\times$ 410 = 410
Maximum stability possible = 2110

$$\text{Stability index} = \frac{850}{2110} = 0.4 \text{ or } 40 \text{ per cent}$$

Comparing the two examples shows that size changes do make a difference. It would be completely wrong to work from the current size of the firm if it were known that, in the period under examination, changes had occurred in size. The beauty of this measure is that it is possible to make genuine comparisons between organisations of different sizes.

One word of caution – great care must be taken with the interpretation of comparative data using the labour turnover percentage or the stability index when it is suspected that some of the firms in the sample have experienced considerable changes of size. Where the change is an increase, the labour turnover measure becomes suspect, and where it is decreased, the stability index loses its power.

An example of how these two measures can tell a different story is illustrated below. The nine hotels illustrated in Table 14.1 display a similar level

LABOUR TURNOVER AND STABILITY · 133

Table 14.1 Labour turnover and stability indices for nine hotels

Labour turnover rate	Stability index
55.2	77.0
62.8	96.5
89.2	75.4
55.0	75.5
92.0	71.2
119.1	71.6
70.8	76.9
69.6	76.6
32.9	71.7

of stability yet at the same time a wide dispersion of labour turnover percentages. What this suggests is that a hotel gets a similar level of service from those who stay, while an unstable element creates turnover percentages very much larger than the overall indicates.

Further reading

Davidson, M.C.G, Timo, N. and Wang, Y. (2010) 'How much does labour turnover cost? A case study of Australian four- and five-star hotels', *International Journal of Contemporary Hospitality Management*, 22, 4: 451–466.

Why read this? It is so easy and tempting to exaggerate the cost of something which is hard to remedy, but here is a genuine attempt to measure these costs. However, the cost and frustration of this problem needs to be seen in terms of the arguments made in Chapters 11, 12 and 13.

PART IV

Human resource management in practice

CHAPTER

15 Administration – the necessary bureaucracy

There is always a basic administrative function to be undertaken; whether this is done by someone called a Human Resource Manager or by someone else, it still has to be done. HRM is often seen as bureaucracy, which is a little unfair. Such sentiments are really a substitute rationale for rejecting a strong internal labour market (see Chapter 11) which is, in itself, perfectly legitimate. The real problem for HRM in the hospitality industry is that the normal unit size is far too small to carry a specific HR Manager, but someone still has to maintain some kind of personnel function. Often this function is delegated to an Assistant Manager, who is responsible for other areas as well, or it is split between two or more people. In the case of large companies, the response of Head Office HRM is to try to lay down guidelines in order to achieve a minimum standard of administration. This structural difficulty could easily be used as an excuse for poor administration, but it is really a very strong argument for actually doing it efficiently. This chapter is full of lists!

Chapter objectives

- to identify the range of tasks involved in administering a workforce;
- to point towards some good habits;
- to show how administration relates to the psychological contract (Chapter 3).

If one takes a close look at the role HR management actually plays in the business, it is possible to identify four points of impact. First, it was suggested that the psychological contract was, at its inception, always imprecise. All the paraphernalia of job descriptions, good interviewing, good recruitment, trial periods, induction etc. are, in effect, trying to make the agreement less imprecise. The more mutual the understanding can be between the new recruit and management, the greater the likelihood that the person will give the performance expected. This is, in effect, the second point of impact – supporting the economic objectives of the organisation by trying to find the most productive people. This cannot be understated, because productivity in this industry is individual productivity. It will come as no surprise that recruitment is a

HUMAN RESOURCE MANAGEMENT IN PRACTICE

prominent feature of the HR function, but it is important to realise that who-ever is doing the recruiting is sitting at the interface between the internal and external markets and in fact controlling that relationship. The response of the external feed back into the internal is through the recruiter because no one else knows what is happening in the external market. The last point of impact is in coping with the fallout when the relationship between management and worker goes wrong. Discipline, grievance handling and disputes procedures don't work automatically – they need handling. Being part of management does not compromise the need to make whatever procedures are agreed on actually work.

None of these four points of impact are actually precisely represented by particular roles, yet they are what HR activities and roles should be doing.

- Making the relationship between manager and workers more precise, par-ticularly in the initial stages.
- Recruiting the most productive people.
- Managing the relationship between the internal and external labour markets.
- Facilitating the resolution of conflict.

It is not that a HR Manager wakes up one morning and decides to make an employee's psychological contract more precise or relate the internal market to the external, but that is what they are actually doing in much of their daily activity.

If this is HR management's role in the organisation, what is the contribu-tion of administration? All that paperwork – files, reports etc. – what is it for? The objectives of good unglamorous administration are:

- to provide sufficient information for management to make decisions affect-ing individuals, groups, departments, occupations and the workforce;
- to promote the feeling of equity of treatment;
- to give individual employees the feeling of confidence that their affairs with the organisation are being administered correctly;
- to promote and maintain the goodwill and reputation of the organisation in the labour market and with external institutions.

What is actually required to achieve these objectives will vary with circum-stances, but there is a bare minimum which any organisation cannot fall below. Every activity has its basic 'good housekeeping' rules and personnel administration is no exception.

Essential good habits in administration

- Maintain all personal files on a comprehensive and 'active' basis. All files to be 'serviced' regularly.

ADMINISTRATION – THE NECESSARY BUREAUCRACY **139**

- Maintain a management information system in respect to manpower.
- Ensure that all the basic 'processes' of personnel are efficiently operated, for example:
  - recruitment
  - selection
  - engagement

- Ensure that all aspects of pay administration are efficient and in line with agreements and laws.
- Ensure that the organisation confidentiality policy operates at all times.
- Pay attention to detail at all times.
- Avoid glitches in the payroll function.

All that talk of motivation in Chapter 4 counts for nothing if the HR Department loses files! News of sloppy administration soon gets around. Beyond a basic duty toward employees, there is an obligation to produce information to assist managerial decision-making. In fact, the quality of aggregate information produced for management is, at least to an extent, dependent on the degree of vigilance over individual files.

Hard data/soft data

In any organisation, the Finance Department produces hard data that is factual data; e.g. cash levels, stock levels, revenue etc. Although this data is open to interpretation when presented together, each piece of data is 'hard'. A person's date of birth in a HR file is hard data. The number of people who leave the organisation is hard data. In contrast, a note on a file which says that Mr X left because he was unhappy with his pay is soft data. It may be true, but there could be other reasons and, in itself, it is open to interpretation – so it is soft. Giving Mr X an appraisal rating of 'excellent' is soft data for the same reasons; it is subjective data.

The importance of distinguishing between hard and soft data is that HR information tends to be a combination of both. Often they are confused and hard data is somehow seen as more valuable than soft. Soft data is subjective data, but that does not mean that it is less valuable. What matters is the integrity with which the data was collected. This means that soft data should not be generated by people with a vested interest in its interpretation. This is where the independence and integrity of HR actually matters.

Principles of designing personnel data collection

- Define the purpose of the data collection, which means defining the activity or behaviour you are interested in.
- Decide whether you are interested in locating the problems within the organisation in relation to this activity or monitoring long-term trends in the activity or both.

140 HUMAN RESOURCE MANAGEMENT IN PRACTICE

- HR data is not designed so that you can take action directly from the data but should be designed to show what the problem is and where it is and suggest what questions you need to ask of those with authority in the identified area.
- Ensure that soft data is collected in an unbiased way.

Day-to-day administration – policy guideline

In concluding this chapter, it might be useful just to list the activities that may require a guideline policy in the area. The list is not comprehensive, and many more activities could be included. The important point in laying down guidelines is not to put people in straightjackets but to give them flexibility while ensuring that people know who does what!

- Documentation (what goes into, who has access to):

  personal files;
  contracts of employment;
  job descriptions.

- Regular procedures:

  recruitment;
  selection;
  employment;
  termination;
  appraisal;
  promotion;
  status change;
  transfer.

- Occasional procedures:

  discipline;
  grievance;
  legal.

- Manning levels:

  performance standards;
  casual labour;
  overtime.

- Pay:

  grade structure;
  incremental structure;
  job evaluation;
  overtime;

ADMINISTRATION – THE NECESSARY BUREAUCRACY 141

deductions;
loans;
advances;
savings plan.

- Benefits:

  sick pay;
  holiday;
  discounts;
  entitlements;
  health plans.

- Training:

  induction;
  skills;
  supervisory;
  statutory;
  management.

- Security:

  locker inspection;
  security checks.

- Relationship with external bodies:

  government;
  education.

- Trade unions:

  recognition;
  agreement;
  bargaining structure.

- Individual recognition:

  seniority;
  long-service awards;
  birthdays;
  retirement.

- Organised employee social activities
- Staff accommodation.

Seen as a list it looks daunting, but if the basic documentation is computerised, then many of the other functions become much easier to administer. The argument here is that if the basic things are done properly, then management strategies related to the business will have a greater chance of success.

HUMAN RESOURCE MANAGEMENT IN PRACTICE

Further reading

Hales, C. (1993) *Managing Through Organization,* London: Routledge.

Why read this? This is a serious management text book which amongst its many merits shows how basic formalisation and bureaucracy are positive aspects of managing effectively.

CHAPTER

16 Pay management

Pay is often discussed in terms of motivation and entwined with other stimuli (as outlined in Part II). It is time to look at pay on its own because it is never neutral. There are three reasons for this. Firstly, it is inseparably linked to effort. Secondly, its distribution is about fairness, a sense of equality and discrimination and thirdly pay is a language everybody understands. Because of this, you can translate anything about effort into a value that can be communicated; everybody needs 'more money', 'makes an effort', 'goes the extra mile'.Similarly, people compare their lot with others and feel envious. These are all readily understandable sentiments. This gives grievances about pay a special legitimacy that others don't have. Problems about the supervisor or some detail of the work are not easily translatable currency; people may simply not understand.

In this chapter we look firstly at how pay is related to leisure (time off work) and secondly how people feel about their pay, and then we go on to a review of how it is distributed. Feelings about pay and the way it is distributed are the bedrock of an organisation's reward system. Acceptance by employees of the way pay is distributed is essential. It is something that must be got right. We look critically at the most common formalised way of regulating pay – job evaluation.

Chapter objectives

- to understand how pay is connected to leisure and convenience;
- to understand how pay can be interpreted;
- to understand how organisations distribute pay through structures and systems;
- to introduce job evaluation;
- to understand the mechanics of doing a pay survey.

Pay and leisure

It is interesting how easy it is for a legitimate opinion to overlook the obvious: the advocates of pay as the prime motivator are, of course, both right and

HUMAN RESOURCE MANAGEMENT IN PRACTICE

wrong. Pay does motivate in lots of ways, but will people go on increasing this effort endlessly as more and more increments of pay are added? This seems doubtful. Common sense tells us that there must be a physical limit, but does it stop before that? Yes, it does. There must come a point when you want to spend your earnings. In other words, at some stage, effort and leisure begin to compete.

The model in Chapter 12 shows that there is strong pressure in the system to keep pay low for a majority of workers and that these workers often work unsocial hours. This does not mean that the leisure equation doesn't apply to them – it does. Leisure pursuits can become a priority over effort at any level of income. It is too easy to think of only rich people having leisure – they have more leisure and more expensive leisure – *but non-work time can be enjoyed, and therefore valued, no matter what the income.*It is worth noting that this whole argument can be turned on its head and leisure used as a stimulus instead of pay. Leisure has its own motivational stimulus as well. If we substitute the word 'convenience' for leisure, non-work time makes sense as a motivational stimulus. The lessons from the relationship between pay and leisure are, first, that more pay increases the quality of leisure but always risks the turn back situation and, second, that convenient employment, which dovetails into domestic financial needs and leisure pursuits, is itself a genuine motivational strategy.

Interpretations of pay relationships

Pay is something that people reflect on through comparisons. My pay compared to:

- absolute value – 'cost of living going up ...'
- my effort – 'I've worked hard for this ...'
- the effort of others – 'he gets the same as me for less ...'
- the pay of selected others – 'I should get as much as ...'
- profits – 'they make enough to pay me a bit more ...'
- status – 'someone of my status should earn ...'
- summing up effect – 'this is your life ...'
- past sacrifices – 'I gave up a lot for this ...'

The fourth interpretation, 'the pay of selected others', is of particular interest. Who are the selected others and why have they been singled out for comparison? If comparison with others is used as a justification for feelings of unfairness or even a pay claim, then it certainly matters who people use for comparison purposes. It is easy to make an invidious comparison which will certainly produce psychological discomfort (see Chapter 5). In fact, workers don't do that. The underlying principle of comparisons is usually similarity of skill. In other words, workers compare themselves with workers who have similar skills and who earn more than they do! This gives a pay claim a touch

PAY MANAGEMENT **145**

of both common sense and strategy. Tradition also plays a hand here. It is for both these reasons that pay leagues tend to remain fairly stable over time, as do company pay structures.

Hospitality workers have no others to compare themselves with if the similar skills principle counts. Thus the hotel and catering industry is an occupational community with a unique set of skills (see Chapter 12). This coupled with the phenomenon of occupational rigidity whereby people change employer to change type of job rather than change type of job with the same employer. This means that comparisons that are made are between employers for the same occupation.

Investigators always end up in a maze when seeking the cause of a pay problem. It is not always the amount and a comparison. There is an alternative suspect which must not be overlooked – the pay system.

Pay and pay systems

Perhaps one of the strongest findings of pay research has been that people have quite separate feelings about pay and the pay system which produces their earnings. By pay system, it is meant the system of overtime, bonus, basic, gratuities etc. used to make up the final pay packet. The model in Chapter 12 talks about the need for flexibility of labour supply, and the pay system plays an important role in this, providing earnings flexibility and, at the same time, acting as a grievance-handling mechanism in relation to the effort-reward bargain.

By what means is a pay system a grievance procedure? The proposition is based on the function of the pay system as a regulator between effort and reward. The particular grievance referred to here relates to the circumstances where the demands of the job exceed normal expectations. An individual in their job adjusts himself to give a level of effort in return for a certain level of reward. When more effort is demanded, the individual expects greater reward. This is not specially negotiated: the pay system simply comes into action and increases the reward. Two simple examples would be: where extra hours are required overtime is paid; or where more production is demanded the incentive system adjusts the reward. In other words, the pay system is the means by which rewards are adjusted in line with fluctuations in effort. An example of the type of pay system which adjusts in this way is the gratuity system.

The gratuity system rewards this form of extra effort through increased tips or a greater share of the service charge. While it would certainly be wrong to infer that staff increase their effort only in response to incentives, it would be unrealistic to suggest that this has no influence, or that in the absence of an adjustment staff would not feel a sense of grievance.

What the pay system is doing is maintaining a balance between effort and reward under fluctuating conditions. In a sense, the gratuity system settles this type of grievance before it is raised, but not before it is felt. The average size of work group in the industry is small and, therefore, such effects are

146   HUMAN RESOURCE MANAGEMENT IN PRACTICE

likely to be felt severely. It is not difficult to see the vicious circle which can follow from this type of situation.

Pay administration

An earlier chapter discussed the potency of pay as a motivator, but whether that is true or not, what is certain is that pay is always philosophical! As an organisation, you are what you pay. This might seem strange at first, but the way an organisation pays its employees contains a philosophy about how they are motivated. An organisation which wishes to retain staff and motivate them through loyalty might adopt a paternalistic pay philosophy, whereby all new employees receive all benefits from their first day – nothing is conditional. Such an organisation might feel that they can best utilise labour and develop flexibility when the labour force is stable. Alternatively, another organisation may have a philosophy of conditional merit, whereby nothing beyond the basic is earned except by merit criteria. This assumes a calculative and competitive motivation in staff. What is being said here is that the way an organisation administers rewards tells a story to its employees about what it assumes is their motivation.

In any organisation, different occupations have a different value to the organisation, have different training periods and have different labour market characteristics. Consequently, there are different levels of reward. The structure of pay differentials is an intimate part of the structure and functioning of the organisation. That the structure is acceptable to those who live it is crucial to the health of the organisation. One thing is certain and that is that the greater the differentials the more salient pay is in the relationship between workers. Simply because pay is distributed differentially by management, it follows, first, that there has to be some overall justification for the differentials; second, that this rationale has to be acceptable to the staff; and third, that questioning the structure is questioning management's authority and judgement. It is suggested in the model described in Chapter 12 that units in the industry are dependent upon the external labour market; therefore, the rationale for whatever internal structure that exists would be that it is the result of market forces.

What is a pay structure supposed to do?

Fundamentally, a pay structure has to be manageable, and it has to be regarded as legitimate by employees. What is meant by a manageable structure? To answer this question, it is necessary to ask what a pay structure is supposed to do. It has four primary functions. First, to ensure that sufficient numbers of people are attracted to the organisation from the labour market. Second, to encourage the internal labour market to function correctly so that incentives exist for promotion and training opportunities. Third, to ensure that feelings of inequity are not engendered. If, for example, a particular occupation was short-staffed because the rate was not attractive to either external or internal candidates and could not be increased without causing problems elsewhere in the organisation, then the structure is not doing its job and is interfering with the operation. Finally, to allow for the development of new jobs evolved through reorganisation or the introduction of new technology.

Normally, pay structures grow up in a haphazard manner as a result of many pressures, such as the labour market, customs and practices, power bargaining and the boss's whim. The result, when looked at from the outside, appears idiosyncratic and illogical. There are likely to be distortions between job content and rewards and distortion between the rewards for different jobs. However, what looks illogical from the outside might make perfect sense to those within. Just because there are distortions it does not imply that management automatically need to impose logic on a pay structure by such means as a job evaluation programme. Two pre-requisites suggest themselves: first, the existing pay structures must have become in some way unmanageable and, second, the employees themselves must feel the inequity produced by the distortion. To change the wage structure in the absence of either of these two conditions runs the risk of creating more dissatisfaction.

Job evaluation

Job evaluation is a formalisation process that attempts to ensure that the pay structure of an organisation is 'seen to be fair'. However, it is not common within hospitality, where the pay structures reflect market forces rather than internal dimensions. Job evaluation is about 'job content' and pay structures. It is not about levels of pay or pay systems, although it is closely associated with both. Job evaluation schemes are about formalising a pay structure, making it rational with the objectives of the organisation. It is a technique by which relative value is given to jobs in order to confer legitimacy upon the pay structure and, more importantly, upon pay differentials. In other words, the work of job evaluation is to change the pay structure, which normally means making it more logical and systematic. By pay structure it is meant the hierarchy of differentials between jobs within an organisation. There are only two questions pertinent to pay structures: 'what is the distance between jobs, and why?' Job evaluation attempts to answer them both by asking 'what should the distance be?'

It is worthy of restatement that job evaluation relates solely to pay structures. Therefore, management must analyse their problems carefully before embarking on such a scheme. They must be able to distinguish a problem of pay structure from other closely related ones such as income, pay systems, pay administration and labour market. This process is in itself complicated by pressure from society norms, which support diversity and equality. So it is not just a case of management's desire to formalise their pay structure to meet organisational goals such as recruitment targets; society may have a strong word in their ear. Once it has been decided that job evaluation is needed, it

148 HUMAN RESOURCE MANAGEMENT IN PRACTICE

might be supposed that it is just a matter of which method. However, this is far from the case, and there are six major factors which have to be considered at the planning stage. These are:

1. the existing pay structure;
2. the selection of evaluators;
3. the appeals system;
4. the entrance of new jobs into the pay structure;
5. the effect of job evaluation on communication in the organisation as a whole;
6. choosing the specific method of job evaluation.

These factors must be considered separately, but they are in reality inseparable.

Be careful

It is generally accepted by experienced practitioners in job evaluation that a new pay structure produced by job evaluation must bear some resemblance to the old pay structure. This is another way of saying that a change in pay structure can never be too radical, unless you want a riot on your hands! The rationale for this is simply that although a pay structure may be illogical to an outsider, it has some meaning to those inside. Employees will have their own views on their own value, their own skill, the skill of others, the authority of others etc., and these perceptions are likely to be assailed by job evaluation.

Here, the relationship between the pay structure and the authority structure is significant. The former supports the latter and, therefore, a change in either will be reflected in the other. Usually, the existing pay structure will be fairly close to the spread of authority; therefore, restructuring has to be done with care. The problem with job evaluation is that it is basically irreversible. The introduction of job evaluation is a watershed for any organisation. There is no going back once logic has entered the system; it cannot be returned at the behest of labour market caprice.

The dynamics of job evaluation: the fundamental issues

Describing a job is not easy, and to do so in a way which places it in relation to other jobs is even harder. Subjectivity and relative judgement abound in this task. Casual analysis suggests that you need attributes of a job that are common to all the jobs in the organisation. Not strictly true, but it is a place to start. The real problems come with the attributes themselves. Take, for example, skill. An obvious way to assess it would be by the input of education and relevant experience (that is, human capital), but there are jobs that require tacit knowledge and skill that cannot be formally taught. Furthermore, skills may be context- specific; hospitality has a set of skills that are different from,

PAY MANAGEMENT **149**

say, seamanship, but with those two industries people will define what is high or low skill. Here is the rub: job evaluation has to define what is skilled or unskilled within the confines of the organisation. A second example of an attribute might be responsibility. The grading would be weight of responsibility, but how to assess this? One simple approach would be 'span of control' (how many employees report). A more sophisticated approach would be 'consequences of error', whereby the job is ranked by what could go wrong and what the consequences would be.Both of these approaches are a variation on responsibility. A further sophistication would be to closely examine the difficulty of decision-making – the complexity and time pressure. Even when the attributes are in place, there is the little matter of degrees to which jobs hold these attributes. Each of these degrees has to be articulated, defined in a way that the level of the attribute can be part of a job description and be a selection criterion. We are concerned here with jobs and not people in them. What job evaluation boils down to is a set of criteria that describe each job but also differentiate them from each other. In other words, we see the comparative value of a job. Here we return to fundamental problem of comparative worth.Why is one job worth more than another? Job evaluation gives an internal explanation based on rational criteria but not on scientific objectivity. Who adds the most value – an unskilled room cleaner or a highly skilled chef? In revenue terms it is often the former!

What are the advantages and disadvantages?

Perhaps the most important benefit of job evaluation is that it gives management a tool by which they can control their pay structure. The accent on job content means that management will be forced to be continually aware of employees' jobs and how they are changing – this can only contribute to the health of the organisation. Furthermore, by giving the pay structure a logical character and a degree of legitimacy, job evaluation overcomes problems of differentials which cause dissent and friction amongst employees. In addition, job evaluation usually promotes more open communication within the organisation; to achieve this, its results must be public knowledge. These, then, are the benefits.

However, all this presumes that the exercise has been carried out successfully, which basically means that everybody is happy with the results. This dependence on the acceptability of the results is the central weakness of job evaluation. It is, in fact, a pseudoscientific technique – its measurement being purely subjective (work study is subjective to a degree). The values it places on jobs and the distances it prescribes between jobs are abstract conceptions. They become 'reality' only if you are prepared to believe them. This is why faith in the system and trust in the evaluators is so vital to the success of any scheme. This weakness does not, however, invalidate the techniques.

A more serious criticism of job evaluation stems from a more general criticism of the true importance of pay structures. One of the major influences on

150 HUMAN RESOURCE MANAGEMENT IN PRACTICE

the pay structure is the labour market, but is there any evidence to show that a logical pay structure is any less susceptible to pressure than an idiosyncratic one? Major movements in the labour market can distort a logical structure like any other, but what is significant is that the sheer logic of systematic pay structures may make it difficult to respond to market pressures. A less organised scheme may have less difficulty in adjusting. Given the basic irreversibility of job evaluation, such rigidity may be a disadvantage. To put it simply, the value which a scheme gives to a job may not be that put on it by the labour market, and sooner or later the two values will clash.

Pay structures and pay systems are different but related

As job evaluation is about job content, it does not concern itself with performance. It is concern for performance that forces a link between the pay grading structure produced by job evaluation and the pay system.

There must be a degree of overlap between pay grades to allow for seniority increments and merit increments. All organisations need some people to stay in their jobs, and such requirements can be met by seniority or long-service increments. As the person is doing the same job, they cannot be regraded; therefore, the top limit of their grade must overlap the higher grade. Similarly, differences in merit should not be suffocated by the lower point of the grade above. Merit can exist without promotion possibilities; therefore, merit increments should be able to overtake the lower points on the grade above. The greater the overlap of grades, the greater is the weight given to the incumbent of the job against the value of the job content.

Pay surveys

It is not uncommon to find managers baffled by the wage survey they themselves commissioned. Complex surveys do require a degree of statistical sophistication and expert interpretation. However, the situation often demands a simpler, less ambitious form of survey.

What has to be accepted at the outset is that labour market surveys are a most difficult type of survey to conduct.

What do pay surveys measure?

Pay surveys measure the differences between occupations and organisations in a defined labour market area in terms of:

- absolute value of pay;
- increase or decrease in value over time;
- the rate of increase or decrease over time.

PAY MANAGEMENT **151**

Obviously, the prime objective must be to find out what other firms are paying in the occupations you are interested in. However, that is not as simple as it sounds. A further objective must be to collect data in such a way that you can understand it and will be able to see the relationships you want. What you are looking for in a pay survey is the state of competition which will be revealed in the relationships between the figures you collect; but only if the information is collected with care.

There are basically three types of pay survey, each with a different capacity.

Photographic shot. The most common form of survey is the one-off photographic shot, where the surveyors collect data just once and for a specific purpose. This type of survey usually collects data on:

a)   The absolute value of pay by occupation and by firm and also, therefore,
b)   pay differentials by occupation and by firm.

Repeated survey. If a survey is repeated at intervals over time it can add other dimensions to the data. Repeated surveys can show:

a)   absolute value of pay by occupation and by firm;
b)   pay differentials by occupation and by firm;
c)   absolute value of the increase or decrease over the time period by occupation and by firm;
d)   change in differentials by occupation and by firm;
e)   the 'rate' of increase or decrease;
f)   differences in the 'rate' of increase or decrease.

Repeated surveys with indexation. The advantage of using indexation is that it shows the direction and rate of change more clearly than absolute figures. The normal practice is to use *one year as the base year* (= 100) and let all other years be expressed as a percentage of that base year. Alternatively, it is possible to use *one occupation* as the base (= 100) and express all other values of pay against the base.

Example 1
Base year 2010 = 100

	2010	2011	2012	2013	2014
Occupation	110	120	120	145	160
Index	100	109	118	132	145

Example 2
Base occupation x = 100

HUMAN RESOURCE MANAGEMENT IN PRACTICE

Index
Occupation x = 110 = 100
Occupation y = 150 = 136
Occupation z = 170 = 154

It is not difficult to see that both types of indexation can be usefully combined. The real value of using indexation is when the surveyor is more interested in the rate of change than in comparing the absolute value.

Some problems associated with setting up a pay survey

Defining the labour market you are trying to measure

If it is a local labour market, knowing the geographical parameters is essential. These are normally approximated by estimates of *travel to work times and cost*. In order to avoid wasted effort, it is a good idea to know who the key firms are who represent competition. If a particular firm is known to be a pay 'leader', they must be included in the sample.

Like with like!

The basis of a survey – that is, its whole validity which allows for interpretation – is that like is being compared with like. If occupational pay is being compared, then the *occupations must be equivalent*. The same occupational title is not enough. In order to ensure occupations are equivalent, either of two conditions must prevail.

1. The survey should use an occupational classification. The importance of this cannot be overstated.
2. The surveyor should have enough knowledge of essential differences between occupations to interpret the data with accuracy.

It is also essential that the *units of measurement are equivalent*: basic pay = basic pay or total earnings = total earnings. Is the survey measuring starting pay or pay at some other point in time?

Understanding the flow systems

At the very minimum, the surveyor must be aware of occupations which are linked in some way. Links can be for a variety of reasons, e.g. occupations which compete for the same people or an occupation which is training for another.

The point about occupations that are linked is that pay differentials can be explained by the nature of the link, and in some circumstances their pay might be expected to move together. The central concern is occupations that fit across both markets (see model in Chapter 12).

Time coherence

In order to interpret your findings, certain additional data is essential:

- the date of the last increase;
- the date on which pay levels are set;
- the frequency of pay reviews.

Interpretation

Given that your survey has been properly produced so that occupational equivalence and unit of revenue of equivalence can be taken for granted, then interpretation is possible. Value and increase differentials can be easily seen, as their interpretation depends on the circumstances. Questions like: 'am I paying too much or too little?' and 'how much more would I need to pay?' should be guided by the figures. It is, however, more difficult to interpret the state of competition from a pay survey. The key indicator is the spread or range of pay offered for the *same* occupation.

Further reading

Furnham, A. and Argyle, M. (1998) *The Psychology of Money*, London: Routledge.

Why read this? The complexities of pay management are legion, but this book is a good place to start.

CHAPTER

17 Appraisal

Everyone wants to know how they are getting on – it's natural. Therefore, feedback becomes part of the interaction between the subordinate and the superior. Knowing 'where you stand' and 'if you are on the right lines' are part of everyday work and, as such, informal appraisal is continuous and part of daily life. That an organisation would want to turn this process into a formal system is quite rational. Rational, but never easy, and it can be a bit of minefield. Each part of the process might be 'on the right lines' but is everybody on board? An appraisal system attempts to ensure some continuity of purpose by checking the validity of individual goals in terms of organisation goals.

Chapter objectives

- to highlight the problems of ambiguity in a system;
- to show how appraisal can realign a person with their role;
- to offer common sense advice on conducting an interview.

There is a fundamental ambiguity inherent in any appraisal system surrounding its purpose: is it an absolute judgement about developing a person's skills and knowledge or is it a relative judgement comparing person X to other persons? If it is a relative process, then pay and promotion enter the scene; perfectly legitimate if that was the intention and was understood by all, but problematic if not. Relative comparisons are natural and important, but they are inappropriate where the primary purpose is to improve an individual.

For a start, everyone not only wants to know how they are getting on but to know this in relation to others. Again, perfectly natural but potentially problematic for a system. It would be obvious to use an appraisal system to rate employees for promotion, but in doing so it may introduce a note of ambiguity in the way the system is perceived by both managers and workers. To illustrate the point, if a worker comes to an interview thinking that its purpose is to discuss the development of skills, they might tell of personal weaknesses. This would not be in their interests if the appraiser considered the purpose of the interview to be to decide on pay in relation to others! All appraisal systems have the potential to disrupt in this way.

An appraisal system can promote effectiveness, job satisfaction and better employee utilisation. It can also promote organisational inefficiency, personal insecurity, distrust and conflict; which way it goes depends on how it is done. Doing it well means, at a personal level, the interviews being conducted professionally and, at an organisational level, by the purposes of the system being clearly defined with natural contradictions resolved. To a large extent, the performance of appraisers is dependent upon the integrity of the system.

Purposes: a case of potential ambiguity

Possibly the best way to understand the purposes associated with appraisal systems is to ask why an organisation would have a formal system. There are a number of reasons.

- To ensure that each job is being done in the way which the organisation wants it to be done; e.g. output standards, the right method and the right priorities.
- To stimulate better performance.
- To assess performance and inform those assessed about how their performance is seen.
- To collate aggregate information on employee capacity. Literally a skills audit.
- To measure the strengths and weaknesses of the selection procedure.
- To measure the relative performance of employees.
- To highlight promotable employees.
- To indicate where skills need to be developed and improved.

Looked at objectively, these purposes seem perfectly reasonable. The problem occurs when they are telescoped down into an interview. 'Why are we here? Is it to fulfil all these purposes?'

What exactly is the character of the interview?

- Counselling – to help the employees to overcome some difficulty?
- Promotion – assessing the potential for another job?
- Training and development – assessing future needs?
- Pay – deciding on how much performance deserves?

An appraisal interview cannot accomplish all these objectives; therefore, to ask it to do so simply renders it ambiguous and ineffective at achieving anything. If ambiguity exists in the system, people will become defensive at interviews and managers will become cynical about the system itself. This is self-defeating.

At the heart of the dilemma lies the absolute nature of a development need. If an employee is not performing properly in a particular area of the work, it matters not a jot whether they are better or worse than someone else. When

156 HUMAN RESOURCE MANAGEMENT IN PRACTICE

it comes to development, relative judgement doesn't count. To remedy a deficiency you have to look at it in absolute terms. This is why appraisal for development and appraisal for promotion don't sit comfortably together.

Resolving the ambiguity

An organisation has to ask certain questions in order to reduce the ambiguity of a system.

- Is the appraisal system part of the control process?
- Is the appraisal system there to allocate rewards?
- Is the appraisal system for developing the needs of employees?

The answer may be yes to all three. It is a question of balance and emphasis. What has to be remembered is that overemphasis on the first two will negate the third almost completely. One approach is to let the control system do its job and let the appraisal system address development issues.

Job and people alignment

Perhaps one of the most fruitful returns which an appraisal system can give is to regularly realign people with their jobs. This is particularly important where the quality of work is both crucial and difficult to measure.

People become comfortable with their jobs over time. A natural bias creeps in which is to give priority to:

1. the visible results of the employee's work which the control system measures;
2. what the employee is good at;
3. what the employee likes doing.

Thus, important points of the work which aren't measured, or work that the incumbent is not good at or doesn't enjoy are neglected. An appraisal interview can find this bias and reintroduce the incumbent to the priorities as seen by higher management. A receptionist may enjoy working with the computer and find it easy; the control system demands regular reports but no attention is given to guest relations. What does management want? Usually it is everything, so it is a matter of realigning priorities. An appraisal system is good at this.

The type of work and the systems

It could be argued that if the output of the job can be measured accurately, then all you need is a control system rather than an appraisal system. This is true only if you ignore the personal needs of the operator. What is also true, however, is that in certain circumstances appraisal systems become more important. These circumstances are:

1. when the job requires a good deal of employee discretion;
2. when personal character plays a large part in the success of the job;
3. when the job has wide scope;
4. when it is difficult to measure the output of a job;
5. when quality is difficult to measure and requires some consensus as to what is 'good';
6. when there is a high rate of technological change.

In other words, where standards cannot be easily measured and where jobs are under pressure to change that is when 'talking a job through' can play a significant role.

Common faults of a system

- That any ambiguity in the system is allowed to enter the interview. There may be confusion over the purpose and meaning of the exchange.
- Setting artificial performance measures to please the system; for example, asking people to effect things over which they have little control.
- The Mr Average syndrome. Appraising employees in relation to some idealised 'benchmark' standard. Using only relative comparisons makes a mockery of absolute performance. If the 'benchmark' person were to leave, everyone's 'performance' would change without any actual change taking place. This syndrome distorts the whole process and leads to complacency.
- Letting relative values dominate objective performance values to the extent that everyone is doing relatively well, but everyone's standards are not good enough.

The appraisal interview

What skills are required?

Two skills are essential to the appraisal interview:

1. *being able to give feedback*. The ability to give 'good news' and 'bad news' without causing exaggeration, overconfidence or resentment;
2. *being able to elicit facts and feelings*. The ability to draw out how the individual sees their job and to distinguish between facts and feelings.

Preparation and strategy

In a very real sense, the skills mentioned above stem from preparation and from strategy. Assuming that the interview will be based on some performance

158 HUMAN RESOURCE MANAGEMENT IN PRACTICE

measures and conduct reports, the interviewer must be prepared to support comments with facts. Support for comments is best achieved by looking at performance from a variety of perspectives – behaviour towards supervisor, behaviour towards colleagues, achievements, quality, quantity etc.

Again, working from the reported performance, it is useful to make a list of good and bad performance indicators. Using this as a guide, the interview should elicit feelings about these aspects of the job. People have priorities, and by seeking their priorities the interviewer may also be finding out what they like and what they don't like. This strategy follows the job alignment principle. How far do the good performance indicators relate to priorities and likes and the bad indicators to priorities and dislikes?

The assumption of the above approach is that disliking something leads to poor performance. While this is true in general, there may be barriers which intervene and cause the dislike or simply prevent achievement of anything. When the interviewer comes across a barrier, they must check that it is real and not just an invented excuse. The outcome of an appraisal interview should be:

- an assessment of performance;
- an assessment of priorities;
- an assessment of barriers to performance;
- an agreed plan of action for the future.

Common faults in the interview

- Saying to the appraisee, 'Overall you were fine, but …' and continuing with a string of negatives.
- Saying, 'Let's start with the bad news – leaving the good to the end.' Always start on a positive note.
- Too much criticism – there is a limit.
- Saying, 'You and I know each other – let's get this form filled in and off to those HRM folk!'
- Entering into negotiation – bargaining and contesting the evidence.

Further reading

Baum, T. (2008) 'Implications of hospitality and tourism labour markets for talent management strategies', *International Journal of Contemporary Hospitality Management*, 20, 7: 720–729.

Why read this? The topic of talent management has not yet sustained real purchase within HRM strategy in hospitality. It is nevertheless relevant here because it is about recognition of talent, which is one function of appraisal. How this recognition can become part of a system is covered by:

Ensley, M.D., Carland, J.W., Ensley, R.L. and Carland, J.C. (2010) 'The theoretical basis and dimensionality of the talent management system', *Academy of Strategic Management Journal*, 9, 2: 9–41.

Why read this? This is a very corporate approach to appraisal which highlights the need for criteria to identify talent but also the necessity of systems and schemes.

CHAPTER

18 Recruitment and selection

The one thing we know about hospitality is that its labour markets are dynamic and volatile (see the model in Chapter 12). It is a specialised market, and what this means is that HRM professionals have to understand the jobs they are recruiting and the market in which potential applicants live. In Chapter 3 we talked about the psychological contract, whereby a set of initial assumptions were put in place by first contact exchanges. In an important sense, the selection interview is where everything starts. This chapter suggests some basic recruitment strategies and some common sense notions of how to select employees. It does not include discussion of psychological testing, which is beyond the scope of this book.

Chapter objectives

- to outline the basic principles of a recruitment search;
- to show basic techniques of job analysis;
- to show the basic technique of selection interviewing.

Know what you want

Recruitment is, at heart, a 'search' process. This process contains four main elements: the hiring standard (what you want); the target market (where you think you will find it); the sources of recruitment (by what means you intend to get it); and the cost (how much you are prepared to invest in the search). Clearly these elements are interrelated with performance in one element determining performance in another. For example, if you are vague about what you want, you will probably misread the market, which in turn might make you choose an inappropriate source or channel, and it will end up costing you more than you thought.

Surprisingly, there are only really three recruitment strategies:

1. *ring the bell* – make your organisation visible in the market by spending money on the search process;
2. *pump up the balloon* – extend the size of the labour market by paying more;

RECRUITMENT AND SELECTION 161

3. *do-it-yourself* – extend the size of the labour market by lowering the hiring standard and offering more training.

Obviously, there are many variations, but what will determine your recruitment strategy will be your approach to the four elements of the search process. Recruitment is not an exact science, but if you get the first element wrong, you may get the next wrong as well. In other words, the key to recruitment is *defining what you want in the first place*.

First, look at the job

This is never easy, because you need to translate a job into a person! Or do you? Eventually, yes, but that is not the first stage. You start with the job because a great deal of the labour market possibilities can be estimated from the nature of the job you are recruiting for. Chapter 12 identified the way in which job characteristics reflect labour market characteristics. The four key indicators are: the level of skill required; how specific the job is to your organisation; whether or not performance standards can be easily measured; and the extent to which personal qualities count in the job. The first two will affect the size of the market, but the latter two represent the possibility of greater individual differences in performance. If standards cannot be formally specified, you are going to get a range of performances. Similarly, if the jobs require personal characteristics, they are going to get a variety of personal differences. Both have the effect of producing a wider distribution of pay in the market. Once personal characteristics and appearance are brought into recruitment, then the nature of the market may change in predictable ways – it could be smaller but contain broader pay levels.

However, the market location is not the only concern. The job has to be described to an applicant that may not know the detail of what the job entails. Job descriptions are only a partial description. The more the recruiter knows about the job – what kind of effort is needed, how easy is it to learn – the clearer will be the eventual contract. In hospitality it is an issue as to how much job knowledge a recruiter needs to be effective.

Now look at the person

Nothing helps the recruitment campaign more than knowing exactly what you are looking for. A word of caution is necessary here because the labour market will not pass up someone who exactly meets an exacting specification. It is always a case of approximation; therefore, the specification must be focused but at the same time couched in terms which allow a range of quality across desired attributes to be accepted. This will allow the selection process to be more efficient.

The device for focusing jobs and people is the hiring standard or hiring specification. The purpose of this device is to specify the desired attributes of the person required for the job. Three central features of a hiring specification are: essential attainments, preferred experience and preferred education and

HUMAN RESOURCE MANAGEMENT IN PRACTICE

training. It is also useful to specify aspects you don't want. In the hotel and catering industry, hiring specifications try to express a balance between technical aspects of the job and personality traits deemed essential. An example of a hiring specification for a receptionist would be as shown in Figure 18.1.

The next step is to ask some questions about your search.

1. What information should be given out?
2. What source of recruitment would be appropriate for the vacancy?

Hiring specification

Job specification: Receptionist   **Department:** Front office team

Age range: 18–30

Physical qualifications: Clear speech

Education and training:

Good general education

Speaks two languages

Computer literate and experienced

Preferred experience:

Occupation: reservationist, receptionist, secretary

Length: one year minimum – three years preferred

Stable mobility pattern

Type of establishment: hotel, hospital or professional office

Size of work group: prefer small work groups

Quality of work: able to demonstrate experience of dealing with people, preferably on the telephone. Should have

good online computer experience, particularly with booking systems

Essential attainments:

Good telephone manner

Computer experience

Disposition:

Able to work under pressure – not panic, not easily bored, flexible, dependable

Circumstances:

Settled accommodation

Contra-specifications:

None

Figure 18.1 A sample hiring standard

The first question depends on the size of the market. Basically, the smaller the market the more specific and revealing the information should be. The second question is a matter of selecting an appropriate source or channel. Again, the size of the market is influential. Trawling through a large market may require a number of sources used simultaneously, but fishing with a fine net in a small market may require something very specific and limited. The sources of recruitment are:

- advertising;
- employment agencies;
- internet websites;
- consultants;
- headhunters;
- outplacement consultants;
- existing staff;
- previous applicants;
- casual callers;
- education systems;
- casual correspondence.

If the vacancy is to be advertised you have to consider:

- choice of media – size of web views, circulation figures, readership dates, publication dates and comparative cost;
- timing of advertisement – when published, best day and resource of personnel department;
- cost effectiveness – display, semi-display and lineage;
- classified sector;
- cost effectiveness of repeats;
- use of logo.

Cost and speed are always a factor. The hospitality industry has a time pressure built into its recruitment functions; therefore, recruitment means fast recruitment. For this reason, the processing of applicants who apply without vacancies becomes a prime source of recruitment. Waiting lists are cheap to maintain.

The employment interview

By far the commonest method of selection is the employment interview. Its popularity persists, despite constant criticism of its effectiveness. Such effectiveness is usually measured in terms of the ability of the method to predict job acceptances by candidates and their performance in the job. Critics cite the case for psychological testing and biodata methods as more valid alternatives because they are based on more solid measurements. Thus, the interview

HUMAN RESOURCE MANAGEMENT IN PRACTICE

is labelled highly subjective and unsuccessful. While this is true, and without denying the merits of alternative methods, the whole of people management could be said to be subjective. Of course, interviews are subjective and require judgement just like most of management. The real problems with the interview are that too much is expected of it and that it is often done badly. Fallible though it is, the method is quick, convenient and, when done well, an effective method of selection.

The objectives of the employment interview

An interview is a conversation with a purpose; in fact, it has several purposes all pursued simultaneously. These objectives can be stated quite simply and are:

- to decide if the applicant is suitable for the job, or, to put it another way, to decide how suitable the job is for the applicant;
- to decide if the applicant will fit into the existing work group and fit into the organisation as a whole;
- to attract the applicant to the job (the interview is part of the recruitment process);
- to communicate the essential expectations and requirements of the job (the interview is part of the induction process).

The structure of the employment interview

Looked at clinically, an interview is an information-gathering, information-distributing, information-evaluating and judgement-forming activity! That makes it sound mechanical, but it does emphasise that judgement is based on information; not pre-conceived ideas but gathered information. Good interviewing is often described as a skill, implying that there is some set technique which is universally good. This is true but only up to a point. Good interviewing technique is simply *some good habits and the skill of asking questions.* Be wary of formulas and set plans! There are dangers in overstructuring an interview. There is, however, a format which combines activities with thought and which constitutes a good habit.

The message of the format shown in Figure 18.2 is that the pre-interview stage and the interview itself are two separate sources of information which should first be *evaluated separately and then together* to form the judgement. Each will tell its own story. Are they telling the same story or different ones? The point here is not to come to judgement on the pre-interview material. Just evaluate it and then combine it with the interview information. Figure 18.3 elaborates on the first figure and highlights how the pre-interview stage generates questions that have to be resolved by the interviewer.

RECRUITMENT AND SELECTION 165

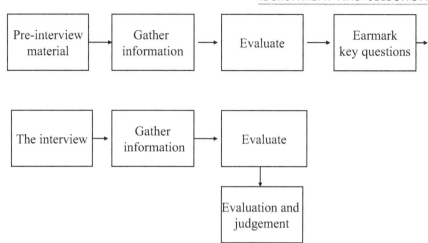

Figure 18.2 Interview format

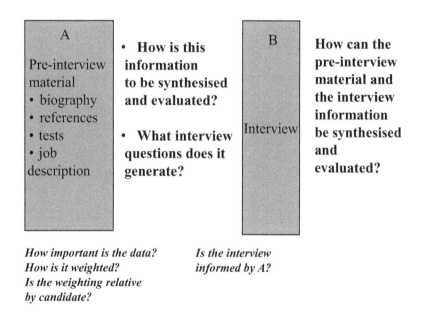

Figure 18.3 Selection interview information dilemma

Should you know the job?

The answer is yes, but it's not an absolute pre-requisite for good interviewing. It all depends on what we mean by 'know' the job. Actual experience of the job or supervising the job brings a certain bias with it, but it is, nevertheless,

HUMAN RESOURCE MANAGEMENT IN PRACTICE

enormously helpful. The task of the employment interview is to bring the character, experience and skills of the applicant and the requirements of the job together in a judgement. To have no knowledge of the job is to render the interview ineffective. Why is job knowledge so necessary? There are three main reasons, which are:

1. it tells the interviewer what questions to ask;
2. it enables the interviewer to assess the relevance of the applicant's career to the job in question;
3. it enables the interviewer to discuss the job with the applicant.

This does not imply that interviewers must have experience of the job. There are other ways of obtaining job knowledge, the most common of which is job analysis. A detailed description of all the duties and responsibilities of a job can be obtained through analysis of the job and laid down in a job description. The job description can then be given to the applicant. The problem with a written job description is that it may mean more to the applicant than it does to the interviewer and is thus not too helpful to the latter in forming questions. However, from a good job description a set of required knowledge, skills and abilities (KSA) can be derived for each duty or responsibility.

*   *Knowledge* – a recognised body of information that is required for successful performance in the job.
*   *Skill* – a competence with a measurable level of performance that is essential to the job.
*   *Ability* – A more general capability.

There are four stages in transferring a job description into an aide for interviewing, which are:

1. job analysis produces a list of tasks;
2. rate the tasks in order of importance;
3. apply KSA to each task;
4. decide which KSAs will influence selection.

Thus, the interviewer has a set of key KSAs at their disposal, but this approach does not directly translate into questions which will help distinguish good from poor.

Perhaps a more direct approach is to combine KSAs with a form of job analysis known as *critical incident technique*. The essence of critical incident technique is that people with experience of a job identify 'incidents' and attach to them examples of good behaviour and poor behaviour. These incidents are more explicit descriptions of behaviour than the simple description of the task. A number of incidents can reflect one task. The key requirement here is a panel of expert people who know the job through experience or supervision to judge important incidents and justify good and bad examples.

RECRUITMENT AND SELECTION   167

An example might be useful here. Suppose the job in question is a hotel assistant manager and you have already obtained a list of tasks and ranked them. One particular task has been identified, among others, as being a useful selector. The task is handling individual guests in respect of personal credit and settling accounts. You now need to identify KSAs.

A critical incident exercise throws up an apposite incident: a room cleaner reports to the supervisor that a room has been severely damaged, with mirrors and furniture broken. The supervisor verifies this and reports it to the assistant manager. The guest is not due to check out for another day.

The first task of the team is to identify what the knowledge skill and ability are in respect of this incident. They would come up with something like:

- Knowledge:

    the legal position;
    the insurance position, including assessment rules;
    rules on credit and procedures;
    current reservation situation.

- Skill:

    to analyse situations into information collection area;
    to be able to devise a set of alternative strategies based on the information collected;
    to be able to think through and anticipate client reactions;
    personal assertiveness;
    recording formally what is required.

- Ability:

    a general ability to confront difficult social situations.

Clearly, this situation will revolve around information on client status, booking situation and damage assessment. The team should then be able to produce a range of examples of what would be good practice and bad practice. The final stage would be to translate this into a situational interview question. This might be either a straightforward 'what would you do?' or the more detailed 'what information would you need to handle this incident?' or 'would you confront the client?'

Given a set of tasks with KSAs attached to them, there are five stages to the procedure of developing something useful to the interviewer.

1. Through the experts, get examples of good and bad practice associated with each critical incident.
2. Allocate incidents to just one KSA that each best illustrates. The process collects the incidents that are selected and rejects those that are not.
3. Translate the salient critical incidents into 'situations' which form the basis of a situational interview. These situations describe an important piece of behaviour in the job.

168 HUMAN RESOURCE MANAGEMENT IN PRACTICE

4. Divide situations into those that would require experience to deal with them and those that would not. In the case of the latter, additional information has to be added to the situation.
5. The question attached to the situation is: 'how would you handle this situation?' It follows, therefore, that some guidance as to what might constitute good and bad performance is required. To do this, the panel of experts has to create a range of answers.

The application of critical incident technique brings the dull job content list to life. By creating situations which illustrate the degree to which an applicant has the relevant KSA, the interviewer gives him- or herself something concrete to assess. One way or another, some knowledge of the job is required by the interviewee. The more realistic and 'alive' the knowledge, the more likely it is that the evaluation of the answers will move from 'yes, they can do it' to 'yes, they will probably do it well'.

Forming questions, question types and strategies

Time is always a constraint in an interview; therefore, it is not to be wasted. The technical goal of the interview is to get yourself into a position to answer four basic questions.

- Can they do the job?
- Would they do it well?
- Will they fit in?
- Are they motivated?

The situational interview places the emphasis on the job and asks: can the applicant match up to good practice in this job? The drawback is that the applicants are being invited to speculate in a way which will make them look good on the basis of what they think the interviewer considers good practice. An alternative strategy is to work solely from the reality of the applicant's past. In other words, the strategy is to probe their previous employment in order to ascertain what the applicant *did*. This approach is applicant-centred rather than prospective job-centred.

If probing the past is the strategy and there is the usual time constraint, then the style of question must be incisive without being intimidating.

Episodic questions

Episodic questions ask the applicant to recall some specific aspect of the past. Table 18.1 contrasts episodic questions with more generalised questions.

The answers to the episodic questions in Table 18.1 will be more revealing because they produce more precise information. Getting facts is not enough.

RECRUITMENT AND SELECTION   **169**

Table 18.1 Examples of general and episodic questions

General	Episodic
Do you like your present job?	What has been the best moment so far in your present job?
Why do you want to work for us?	Where were you when you made the decision to apply to us?
How do you feel about moving to this part of the country?	What happened in your domestic life when you last relocated?
Do you find dealing with the staff easy?	What happened last time you had to deal with an openly uncooperative employee?

Episodic questions must invite the obvious rejoinder – why did you do that? Or – what alternative did you consider?

However, an interview consisting solely of these types of questions would eventually intimidate and would leave the interviewer with a lot of small 'bits' of information to piece together.

General and open questions

A severe limitation of episodic questions is that they can easily miss the big picture. Motivation is part of that big picture. No one question will give you a clue; an impression has to be formed from a multitude of stimuli. One clue to motivation is the applicant's references and priorities. Here, the general open-ended question can be useful.

- 'Did you enjoy college?'
- 'Tell me about your present job.'

Moving from the general to the episodic, a good strategy is to open with a general question which simply defines the area to think about and then follow it with an episodic question with the appropriate follow-up, as shown below. The technique is called funnelling.

- 'Tell me about your present job.'
- 'What aspect do you most enjoy?'
- 'Can you give me an example of when that aspect went particularly well?'
- 'Why do you think it worked well on that occasion?'

Here, the questioner has gone from the general and, working from the responses, funnelled down to a specific piece of behaviour.

Closed questions

These can be useful to clarify what is already known: 'how long did you spend in sales during your training?', 'You left college at 21?'

Does the job make a difference to the strategy?

Clearly it should! Interviewing a prospective assistant manager and interviewing a prospective chef cannot be the same task. Similarly, interviewing someone for a job to which they aspire but of which they have no actual experience must be different from interviewing someone who has done a similar job before. In this case, the main thrust of the task is different. First, you are looking for managerial ability; second, to verify qualifications and skill; third, to assess potential and ability to learn; and finally, to verify experience.

Perhaps the key difference is whether the job is one requiring managerial skills or manual skills. Clearly, as management is action-orientated, the situational interview or questioning based on action taken in the past might be appropriate. This type of behaviour-orientated questioning is not too appropriate when the job involves manual skills.

For manual skills, it is advisable to have checklists of skills you require and ask the applicant to record this level of competence before the interview. Table 18.2 is an example of a culinary questionnaire.

Table 18.2 Sample of culinary questionnaire

What is your strongest area?
Do you have any banqueting experience? Any insecure fields?

	Which of the following can you cook?	*Which have you cooked in your last job?*
Preparation of pâté	☐	☐
Galantine	☐	☐
Mousseline de sole	☐	☐
Chaudfroid sauce	☐	☐
Lobster mousse	☐	☐
Bouillabaisse	☐	☐
Consommé	☐	☐
Brioche	☐	☐
Praline	☐	☐
Butter sculpture	☐	☐
Ice sculpture	☐	☐
Chocolate modelling	☐	☐

Pre-interview material – do leopards change their spots?

The longer you spend with this material the better. Normally, the kind of pre-interview information available to an interviewer falls into four categories: personal circumstances; employment experience or career; education; and references. They should be addressed separately then judged for coherence. Do they tell a story? What information is missing?

In reviewing the material on personal circumstances, the key question would be: 'how do the personal circumstances fit with the demands of the job?' Also: 'what might be the effect of the job on these personal circumstances?', 'What change, if any, is implied?'

In reviewing education and formal qualifications, the obvious question is: 'are they appropriate and sufficient?' References are more difficult to handle. More than any other aspect of the process they carry the assumption that the past indicates the future, that performance in one job has some continuity with the next.

Do leopards change their spots? This is the usual unspoken question which passes through the interviewer's mind while scanning a career history. Indications of work stability and skill accumulation can be obtained from a career history. The important point is that judgements are not made at this point but questions arise to be covered in the interview.

Evaluating between applicants

There is one safe rule when several applicants are being considered, which is evaluate each one separately before you begin to compare their relative merits. This maxim is true whether or not you've used a structured interview.

For each applicant you will have four sets of information to evaluate:

1. domestic circumstances;
2. previous career;
3. organisational compatibility;
4. suitability for the job.

The advantage of using a structured interview technique based on KSAs, or KSA attached to situations, is that you can compare the performance and response of each candidate against each KSA and situation. However, a holistic evaluation of each candidate must precede any comparisons.

Biases and traps

Perhaps the most helpful hint that can be given to anyone attempting to develop and improve their skill at interviewing is to be aware of the natural

HUMAN RESOURCE MANAGEMENT IN PRACTICE

biases and common traps associated with this activity, examples of which are shown below.

- Favouring negative information over positive information. Selecting a poor performer will be noticed, but missing a good one will go undetected; therefore, screening for negatives tends to be given more emphasis than looking for positives.
- Exaggerating the importance of aspects of the job that you have no knowledge of.
- Letting an impressive attitude make you forget to ask some essential questions about skills and knowledge.
- It is easy to become too systematic and overstructured. Applicants can sense this and anticipate your questions. When this happens you both begin to 'tango'.
- Letting first impressions (good or bad) overrule the evaluation of evidence from the interview.
- Making a judgement on the basis of the pre-interview material, which either the interviewer spends the whole time trying to verify or which simply renders the interview pointless.
- Perhaps the most common and damaging fault is simply to make a decision too soon, often during the interview itself. It needs an effort to train oneself into the habit of always reserving judgement until all the information has been gathered and evaluated.

Some good habits

Often the obvious is taken for granted and thus overlooked. It goes without saying that applicants should be put at their ease. Anxiety, however mild, is a barrier to communication. Space can be intimidating. Thus, inappropriately large rooms and placing the applicant and interviewer wide apart all tend to intimidate. Some writers argue that the interviewer's desk is a barrier and that both parties should sit side by side. The problem with this solution is that it is harder to take notes on your lap and, of course, notes must be taken. Here is the interviewer's main physical problem – how to concentrate and take notes at the same time. The worst position to be in is finding yourself unable to recall an answer to a key question when you are evaluating at the end. Last, but not least, allow yourself time. Not just for the interview but time to appraise the pre-interview data and time to contemplate your decision.

Some bad habits

Two habits that commonly undo good intentions are, first, trying to see too many people in too short a time. In such circumstances, the squeeze is on time for evaluation and judgement. Second, interruptions are preventable and, if

RECRUITMENT AND SELECTION 173

they occur, unforgivable, and that includes during the time you have set aside to think over the applicant.

Further reading

Eder, R.W. and Ferris, G.R. (1989) *The Employment Interview: Theory Research and Practice*, London: Sage.

Why read this? If you are prepared to bypass modern ideas of psychological testing and go back to fundamentals, this book captures the basics and points to future research in a comprehensive and easily understandable way.

CHAPTER

19 Grievance and dispute management

The problem of grievance procedures is that nobody loves them! The problem is that they are, for managers, so easy to disregard. In a sense, the first situation is a result of the latter. Managers find it all too easy to attribute grumbles to troublemakers or disputes to the 'six of one, half a dozen of the other' category, before investigation. To some, 'good people' don't have problems – but they do. To many managers, the formal griev-ance procedure is an unwanted rival to their 'I'm always approachable' authority. Given the complexity of negative behaviour discussed in Chap-ter 5, some sympathy is due to management in this respect. However, managers cannot simply look the other way or rely entirely on their own busy resources.

Chapter objectives

- to understand patterns of conflict behaviour;
- to recognise the issue of consistent junior management behaviour;
- to understand how a grievance procedure is designed.

At any one time in any organisation there will always be a degree of dissat-isfaction, and while it is impossible to eradicate grievances altogether, it is clearly management's task to minimise and contain such conflict. The prob-lem facing management is not simply a matter of the complexity of grievances but that they exist at numerous levels. To put it simply, there are individual, group and workforce grievances. Obviously as the scale of the problem varies the means of prevention and resolution also vary to scale.

Prevention is better than cure, but if you have a problem there must be some means of settling it without damaging the operation. The key elements in prevention are knowing the patterns of conflict (labour turnover, absen-teeism, stoppages etc.); the behaviour of supervisors and junior managers; and the organisation's operating policies, particularly HRM policies. The key element in resolution of conflict is the operation of an authentic dispute and grievance procedure.

Prevention tactics

Know the pattern of conflict behaviour: the case of high labour turnover

The hospitality industry has a reputation for high levels of labour turnover – the facts confirm this. The levels are so high that consideration of any other form of conflict behaviour tends to be subsumed under this one problem. Two cases can be made that mitigate high levels of labour turnover; these are the need for numerical flexibility to match variations in demand and the need for skill accumulation by personal mobility (Chapter 12). Accounting for these cases still leaves an awful lot of conflict-related labour turnover.

The first step to prevention is to recognise the type of problem that you have, which includes separating the preventable from the inevitable. In relation to preventable conflict, three areas of concern can be identified from research.

1. *The arbitrary behaviour of supervisors and managers*. Because of the shift system and because standards are subjectively defined, employees face more than one supervisor, each with their own ideas about what they regard as good performance. Inconsistency is difficult to work with. This may be the background pattern of quitting, based on what is seen as unfair action by managers.
2. *The induction crisis*. The induction crisis is endemic in the industry. Workers leave employers within a very short period because either the job is not what they thought it was going to be or it is incompatible with their non-work life. While acknowledging that the pressure of the recruitment function is often extreme, there is always a premium on getting things as straight as possible at the outset. As a generalisation, recruiters concentrate on the person's ability to do the job but neglect to find out whether the person has *realistically thought out the job in terms of their domestic life for themselves*. Often an interviewee makes a mistake which costs the employer time and trouble.
3. *Distribution of effort and rewards*. It is suggested that because productivity is through individual effort and does not increase with length of service, there is no point in rewarding seniority. While true in general, this argument loses some of its force on the ground. People expect to be rewarded for producing more or staying longer. With a workforce that contains both a transient population and a stable population, the lower levels of management are confronted with an enormous problem of how to distribute rewards and effort in such a way as to turn the transient population into permanence while not upsetting the already permanent employees by denying privileges to them. Matters like the distribution of days off have no economic impact but have enormous significance for operational health.

Know the issue of the junior managers and supervisors

In the front line of people management are the supervisor and the junior levels of management. It is their behaviour that, to a large extent, determines the general level of morale and incidents of discontent. Given how imprecise labour contracts are for service workers, there is a greater than normal probability of misunderstanding and misinterpretation. It is difficult to manage service workers through a set of ambiguous rules. What is more, the occasion of shift overlap means that most workers have more than one manager, which leads to a problem of inconsistency. All this points to the need for the training of supervisors and managers in people-handling skills. Uniformity would be impossible and undesirable, but a degree of consistency in actual skill can only be beneficial.

Policies that help

- *Knowing the house rules*. There are always some house rules, and while it is usual to get them across through the induction process, people forget. Many problems occur over a misinterpretation of rules; therefore, access to the rules and, if necessary, an independent interpretation (possibly by the Personnel Manager) would cut off grievances before they start. It is the 'is he allowed to change my day off?' syndrome.
- *Individual differences*. As productivity is individual productivity in this industry, it is wise to select carefully to avoid friction based on effort comparisons.
- *Distribution of effort and rewards*. Give guidelines to departmental managers on distributing effort and rewards. Make clear divisions between the status of those under training and those accepted as competent performers. Give clear guidelines on the privileges of long service.
- *Irregular hours of work*. Even if consumer demand is irregular, work can be organised on a continuous basis. Waiting around for work simply breeds gripes.
- *Promotion and training*. Well-organised training and published opportunities.
- *Pay system*. Easily understood and with legitimate differentials.
- *Pay and benefits*. Competitive.

The goal of these policies is to try to eliminate unfair arbitrary management action, unstable and irregular work, inadequate employee status and recognition. The above policies don't, themselves, promote harmony, but they are the bedrock on which it is built.

Grievance and dispute procedures

There is a certain irony in the fact that neither managers nor workers are enthusiastic to use the formal grievance procedure. Managers see it as a slight

GRIEVANCE AND DISPUTE MANAGEMENT 177

on their authority and workers don't trust the system, because it always supports management authority. Looked at objectively, if workers do take their grievances to the system they are in fact affirming management authority. Grievance procedures are about justice, rough justice possibly, but justice nevertheless.

The real merits of formal procedure are, first, that by bringing the grievance out into the open they force resolutions to be on the lines of some fair principles or precedents. Second, this form of resolution is healthier for the organisation in the long run than the alternative form of resolution that is an informal settlement. Informal approaches are necessary and sometimes preferable but not for everything. The danger of informal systems is that they use 'favours' and 'reciprocity' as the basis of resolution which are, by their very nature, secret and open to misinterpretation. There is plenty of evidence to show that when the informal settlement system dominates, it ends in an expensive mess with unofficial privileges having to be bought out! Settling a grumble with a bit of extra overtime solves nothing!

Impact of a procedure upon a grievance

- It helps to identify those to whom the grievance should be put and those who may be approached for assistance.
- It may help to clarify the issue if the grievant has to write it down or explain it to a representative.
- It may help to obtain appropriate information.
- It may speed up resolution in so far as it specifies time limits and ensures only those with the appropriate authority are involved.
- By requiring that records be kept, it lessens the chances of ambiguous customs and practices becoming involved.
- It reduces the level of emotion involved.

Designing a procedure

There is a dilemma at the heart of any judicial procedure, and grievance and dispute procedures are no different. The problem is that *speed of resolution* is incompatible with *consistency of justice*. Anybody with a problem wants it resolved as soon as possible. This is natural. If everything were solved quickly that would mean everything would have to be settled at a low level of authority. This would mean inconsistent judgements, which would, themselves, eventually become the source of conflict. Alternatively, if one person made all the judgements, they would be consistent but dangerously slow. This is the design problem of all procedures – how to reconcile speed with consistency.

Fundamentally, grievance procedures consist of a number of dimensions. These are first a number of stages following a set order. At each stage there is an attempt to resolve the grievance. Second, there are levels of authority which are superimposed onto the stages of the grievance procedure. For example, the first two stages may attempt to resolve the grievance at supervisory level, after which the remaining stages move to an ever higher authority level. The big element here is the terminal stage where the grievance must be resolved. Third, at any stage, representation or arbitration may be superimposed. Fourth, there is the matter of formality; the degree to which the procedure is written down and rigidly applied. Finally, there are fixed time limits on the duration between each stage in order to prevent unfair delays.

Key issues in designing a procedure

These are the issues that have to be addressed in setting up a procedure.

- Basic structure – number of stages.
- Place of the terminal stage.
- Time limits on stages.
- Roles of participants.
- Recording of procedure stages.
- Scope of the procedure.
- Representation.
- Procedure differentiation (some problems may require different procedures).

None of this will work without someone making it work. This is usually a role for HRM. Where a union is recognised, it is essential to specify the point in the system when union representation takes place and the point where the dispute can go to arbitration. These matters are the subject of negotiation.

It must be said that whatever thoughts managers have about grievance procedures, in many labour regulatory systems they are compulsory!

PART V

The wider perspective

CHAPTER

20 Developing Human Resource Management (HRM) strategies

This chapter does not advocate any particular HRM strategy; it only points out a questioning process of development. It does, however, build the process on the assumption that it is the whole package – that is, everything about a job that counts. The philosophy of the process is simply that a strategy is more likely to work if you believe in it, and you will believe in it if you find your own judgements convincing. The process advocated here is designed to help you think through to that conviction.

Chapter objectives

- to understand the importance of coherence in HRM strategy;
- to understand what HR policies make up strategy;
- to understand the relationship between HRM strategy and the hospitality labour market.

Corporate HRM

There is undoubtedly a HRM movement in corporate life – uncodified but nevertheless an observable trend towards an emphasis on the long term, on getting commitment from people, and encouraging flexibility and quality in general. Having argued that the hospitality industry is, in some ways, unique, does this mean that it is, therefore, outside such a movement? The answer is no, because the HRM movement itself is, to a degree, a reaction to labour market forces – an experience not unknown to the hotel and catering industry. Table 20.1 summarises the direction of the drift towards HRM in the future.

The direction of movement is towards professional planning and long-term thinking.

Strategy and coherence

It will be recalled that right at the beginning of this book there was a lot of talk about the 'immediacy' of the hospitality industry – the focus on the here and now. Yet, here we are near the end talking about strategy. In fact,

THE WIDER PERSPECTIVE

Table 20.1 An overview of corporate HRM

Area of activity	From	To
Time perspective	Short term	Long term
Planning	Reactive	Pro-active
Management-worker psychological relationship	Compliance	Commitment
Evaluative criterion	Cost minimisation	Maximisation of labour utility
Motivation	What motivates	Make it all work (employment packages)
People perspective	Groups from which individuals emerge (have we got a waiter who would make a good X?)	Individuals and their group context (X will work well, be happy and grow in that group)
Selection	Looking for good people (we know the type of person we want)	Examine the job content as well as looking for good people (let's get the job right first, then go for what we want)
Functionalism	Clear boundaries	Integrated with operations
Communication	Walking the job, assessing morale	Attitude surveys
Management skills	Measuring competence	Researching and prescribing 'how'

there is nothing incompatible here. True, strategy is commonly associated with the long term, but it *always embraces the immediate*. It is a fatal flaw to think of strategy as long term and in broad outline. Real strategic thinking and planning starts from where you are now and projects where you want to go to – that's the hard bit; the vision bit! If there is a real criticism to be made of HRM, it is its failure to achieve coherence; effective HRM strategy – that is, one in which all policies face the same direction and tell the same story. If you haven't got HRM policy coherence in the present, then you will more than likely carry it into the future; it is difficult to but impossible to rectify.

In an earlier chapter we discussed that terrible question – what motivates? It is of perennial importance but so difficult to answer. One reasonably safe bet is to bypass all the issues on motivation and to say that whatever you are doing to motivate your staff only has a chance of success *if it makes sense to the individual employee*. If your HRM strategies are coherent, then the individual

DEVELOPING HUMAN RESOURCE MANAGEMENT   183

is more likely to 'sense' what you are doing than if they are being pulled in two different directions at the same time. Giving workers a gleaming new canteen, plenty of scope in their work, harsh supervision and poor pay is not telling the same story; neither is good pay, no autonomy, poor conditions and good supervision. They cannot have everything! Maybe, but if what they have points in the same direction – if it is coherent – then management's motivational exhortations may stand a better chance of getting a response. If an individual is given close supervision and is expected to show initiative, or has insecure tenure of employment and is expected to be committed to the organisation, such contradictions are often only apparent to the individuals concerned, but they undercut management's efforts to motivate. The case for coherence in HRM strategies is that eventually the employee will recognise it and will be able to 'make sense' of what is expected of them. In other words, whatever you do is more likely to work if all the messages tell the same story. This gives us one criterion by which we might judge HRM strategy – is it coherent? The failure to think and plan in detail. In a sense, trying to answer unanswerable questions like what motivates and what the industry needs in terms of specific workforce requirements have prevented management from trying everything and from trying to give everything a coherence.

If it is a game of chance and you don't want to bet on all the horses, at least you can make it a handicapped race! Applied motivation in the future is likely to be about putting attributes together into employment and motivational packages which tell a story to the worker. Without doubt, the technique of the future will be employee attitude surveys. If convenience is going to be a major factor in the decision to work in a leisure society, then 'motivational packages' will be built with regard to how people live as well as what they do at work. The industry values part-time workers because they are convenient to the economics of labour supply, but such workers will have to be valued for much more than this. They are at the cutting edge of productivity. Time and effort spent in motivation here is well spent. Perhaps the future is organising different employment packages for skilled full time, unskilled full time and unskilled part time, irrespective of what job they do.

Creating a vision for HRM

Usually the word strategy is associated with the word planning. This is correct but not sufficient. Strategy means more than designing a plan of action for the future, which requires clear objectives. It also means thinking beyond tactics to solve a problem. Plans require a vision and attendant objectives. The vision for human resources needs the bigger perspective – that of the business as a whole. In a very real sense human resource strategy is a response to business strategy. The implication of this is that human resource managers have to interpret business strategy and from that develop their own vision of what the human side of an organisation should look like. Having said that, organisations have a life of their own that is semi-independent of current

THE WIDER PERSPECTIVE

business strategy. It would be unwise to change your organisation every time you change strategy; at least in the short term.

The creation of a vision is never easy. Common sense and 'reality' get in the way, but we move towards what we can see; therefore, thinking in terms of 'ideal' types and models can be helpful. 'I want cheap staff with wonderful positive attitudes and high skills' is a dream not a model. A model sets out how stable you want the organisation to be, what levels of skill match the commercial objectives of the business and positions the wage levels within the local labour market. The advantage of an imagined model is that it can be compared to the present reality, thus revealing what needs to change and what needs to be valued as it is.

For the business, it may well be that the objectives come from alternatives derived from market information. Consequently, strategy comes from the pursuit of business targets. This is not quite the case with HRM strategy. Here the concern is with continuity and change, and in this respect HRM strategy is more architectural in tone. The central element to all HRM strategy is – 'what do I want my organisation to look like in terms of stability, level of skill,labour market position and reputation in the future?'

HRM is concerned with people, skills, motivation, knowledge, how work should be organised, control and authority. These are the building blocks that make up any organisation; their quality and quantity are interrelated and interdependent. Consequently, any vision and consequent design must examine the interconnections between all these parts of the organisation.

HRM strategy and the business

A shorthand way of describing how HRM strategy is related to business would be to ask and respond to the following questions.

- How many workers are needed?
- What should the proportion be of fixed to variable employment?
- What types of skills does the business need?
- What type of people would work effectively in the business?
- What is the desired organisational culture?

Shorthand it might be, but there are no short, easy answers. The response to these questions depends on two factors in the business environment: the pattern of demand by customers and the level of technological change. Casual analysis of the hospitality industry would suggest that the first factor would dominate and the traditional nature of the industry make the second less important. The truth is not so simple; both these factors inform the process of human resource strategy development.

Review the pattern of demand

The chapters on labour economics and on hospitality labour markets (11 and 12) tell us something of great importance – that the industry is infused with variable customer demand. More importantly – that demand fluctuates in the very short term. This means that to be productive management has to match labour supply accurately to variable demand for labour, which means a decision on the proportion of fixed to variable labour. This has implications for recruitment, retention and pay policies and raises the issue of subcontracting labour.

Review the pattern of technological change

It is important to be clear about what is meant by 'technological' in this context. Here the word is used to describe any work process and not necessarily something done by a machine. To change the service in a restaurant from waiter/waitress service to a self-service buffet is a change in work process and is as much a technological change as replacing manual work by machine.

The *technological assessment* which precedes HRM strategy development has, itself, three components: the type of change, the labour market implications and the control implications – each has a different significance for strategy.

Type of technological change

Looking into the future, what rate and type of change do you envisage?

- Steady state (i.e. no change).
- Gradual change built on existing knowledge and skills.
- Gradual change based on new knowledge and skills.
- Incremental change built on existing knowledge and skills.
- Incremental change built on new knowledge and skills.
- Revolutionary change.

Examples of incremental change might be computerised reservation systems, sous vide and microwave cookers. The impact of these changes is not just on the numbers of people employed but on the type and depth of skill required. Radio-controlled communication between restaurant and kitchen to process customer orders is another example of incremental change. What is important to recognise is that these forms of change do not fundamentally change processes and only add new skills to those already skilled. By contrast, the internet has revolutionised not just reservation processes but also marketing strategies and should really be considered as revolutionary change because it introduces new knowledge and skills into hospitality.

Technology and the labour market

In our Chapter 12 we established that the nature of jobs determines their labour market characteristics; therefore, what has to be assessed is the nature of the jobs to be done because such an assessment is the primary influence on future recruitment policies.

What has to be assessed for each work category is:

- the degree of specificity to the organisation;
- the level of training, education and experience;
- how far personal characteristics count;
- how far knowledge can be substituted by information.

Most of the basic skills of hospitality are not specific to any organisation and many low-skilled jobs (which are vitally important) can be learnt easily and quickly. The only differences are in the level of skills required by the range of quality services offered. For many jobs in the industry, individual personality counts and therefore it becomes a selection criterion. Most importantly for human resource management in hospitality and any other industry is the inevitable trend of access to information as a substitute for conferring with someone with knowledge. If everything can be found on the internet, there is no need for a role such as the concierge – at least in theory. In practice, hotel guests trust the information they receive from a person in a position of authority such as the concierge.

Technology and control

In Chapter 2 we discussed how the nature of a job influences how management applies control. The assessment here is primarily concerned with how far performance standards can be measured and what value management places upon employee autonomy and initiative.

Thinking about strategy

Strategy is essentially about being clear about what you want; this emphasises the importance of managerial 'will' in strategy. The important question here is what knowledge do you need to start thinking strategically? In Chapter 3 we talked about managerial knowledge and ho w it can be categorised. In terms of strategy thinking, it would be obvious that contextual knowledge with its broad perspective would be most applicable, but strategic thinking is not simply about the wider perspective. All the categories from situational through architectural count. You have to be aware of what is happening on the ground now to be able to think about the future.

But, perhaps the best way to understand the process of developing HRM strategy is to ask yourself key questions about people, skills, group orientation,

DEVELOPING HUMAN RESOURCE MANAGEMENT

the organisation as a whole and the labour market. By asking questions you challenge the everyday assumptions you make about these fundamentals. We should start by taking an overview of the organisation, and here the key question is clear – *how stable do I want the organisation to be?* Within this question are number of issues to be resolved.

- What fluctuations in demand are anticipated?
- What type of technological change is in the pipeline? And what does that mean for training capacity and cost?
- Existing skills are not very specific to the organisation and I can just buy them in the market, so I can avoid high recruitment costs.
- Do I want loyalty and commitment?
- Will I get an emphasis on quality if I offer security?
- Recognise that the culture and values of the workplace will be continuously reinforced and will, therefore, be stronger. Guests like to see familiar faces, but is there a downside to this?

When thinking about people, the most common question in hospitality concerns the debate on the value of 'the right attitude' over skill, which leads to other questions.

- How strong is my training capacity? Will people be prepared to pass on their skills to others – willingly?
- How do we identify a service orientation?
- Do I need to incentivise training?
- What is the basis of motivation I need for the performance I want?
- Should I emphasise individual merit or group orientation in my motivational policies?
- Where can I find the skills and attitudes I need?

This leads directly to thoughts about the labour markets. The plural here is deliberate because at the strategic level you must think broadly about recruitment.

- Will I be able to find the skills at a price I'm prepared to pay from existing markets?
- How far can jobs be substituted by people with different skills so I can look in other markets?
- Do I want my organisation to be seen as a good employer in the market place?
- How much do I value the 'fresh air' principle?
- Do I need to protect some skills from fierce market competition by constructing a strong internal labour market?
- Do I have the internal training capacity to reproduce the skills I need?

Again, in addressing these questions you are in fact debating the strength of your internal labour market against the opportunities in the external market.

THE WIDER PERSPECTIVE

You are also thinking about job content and the possibility of substitution. Your answers to these questions may well lead you to look at different labour markets and possibly alter training policies. To some experienced recruiters, the argument of the model of the hospitality labour market that hotel and catering units almost always exist in a labour market surplus might strike a discordant note. Running around hoping to keep up with the labour turnover doesn't 'feel' like a surplus. Yet it is. The labour market is tough enough without making it harder for yourself with stereotyped notions of what you want. The search for 'good people' is not helped by a myopic vision of 'willing flexible souls'. Looking for good people means constantly looking at job content. It is not just the person to fit the job but the job itself, to allow the person to be maximally effective. If a genuine shortage exists in the labour market, then management are forced to look at job content, but a modern approach to HRM embraces this as naturally as expert selection procedures. When it comes to evaluating competence and effectiveness, the focus is on job content rather than the personal qualities anyway. Why not make it a central focus in recruitment and selection?

What about the means?

Once you have decided what you want and why you want it, and have refined this down to some objectives, then one additional consideration arises – by what means are these objectives to be achieved? Obviously, the actual means used will depend on the objectives, but broadly speaking, labour strategies can be implemented in a variety of ways:

- through policies, procedures, systems and plans;
- by altering the organisational structure;
- by appointing specific people to implement objectives;
- by making tactical interventions without altering policies or structures.

Thinking the matter through is one thing but once you reach the point of considering means then simultaneously you have reached the point when you have to consider how to communicate the strategy. The great danger with a strategic matter is that it is long term and it is about change so there is simply more time available for misinterpretation by the workforce. In other words, whatever the strategy, the communication of it, both intended and unintended, must be thought through. So far, the only criterion for judging a labour strategy has been coherence, but as everything depends upon the authority of management, this too could be a minimum requirement of any strategy – that it enhances the authority of management. One of the more tedious debates which permeates the industry and vocational education is whether the skills of managing are more important than knowledge of hospitality operations. The argument is destructive because both are necessary and complementary. Paying attention to the skills of managing has the advantage of overriding not only technical knowledge but also functionalism (marketing, personnel, finance etc.). Good practice in HRM assumes that everyone who manages has the skills to do so.

Further reading

Lepark, D.P. and Snell, S.A. (1999) 'The human resource architecture: toward a theory of human capital allocation and development', *Academy of Management Review*, 24, 1: 31–48.

Why read this? This paper brings together skill levels, productivity and labour market characteristics to show how these factors configure the structure and scope of HRM functions within organisations. To see how this applies to hospitality try:

Riley, M. and Szivas, E. (2009) 'The valuation of skill and the configuration of HRM', *Tourism Economics*, 15, 1: 105–120.

CHAPTER

21 Managing in an international environment

Hospitality organisations live in an environment that is invariably international in character; the staff are likely to be multinational and multi-lingual, the organisation may be part of a chain and some of the customers will most likely be tourists. It is these circumstances that constantly remind us that we live in a globalised environment and tend to see globalisation as a seemingly unstoppable, inevitable force. This has the potential to make us forget that we all live and work in a local environment where local commercial competition and labour markets actually matter. However, as local labour markets are regulated by national labour laws, the issue for global human resource management is to understand comparative labour regulation – that is, the differences between national regulation systems. By contrast, for the manager of a hospitality organisation, it is a case of understanding how the national labour regulation they live under affects local conditions and therefore local human resource policy and practice.

Chapter objectives

- to understand why an international perspective on HRM is important;
- to understand the dimensions of a labour regulation system;
- to appreciate the fundamental issue of pay in cross-border management;
- to understand the basis of nationalisation policies and immigration.

Taking an international perspective

In a broad sense the rationale for an international perspective is obvious due to the following:

- the influence of national regulations (labour laws) on the policies and practices of HRM;
- business is now international;
- we are managing a diverse workforce made up of people from different nationalities with different national cultures;
- the existence of cross-border management.

MANAGING IN AN INTERNATIONAL ENVIRONMENT   191

These issues are not abstract; they are part of daily life and need to be, at least, appreciated if not known in detail.

National regulation systems

What an international perspective means for human resource management is under-standing the fundamental structure of labour regulation that pervades all national regulation systems. There are important differences between countries. Govern-ments have different political leanings, but all systems, in any society, address the same problems and are there to maintain order between capital and labour.

Labour regulation is essentially a set of rules laid down in law and a set of practices laid down by norms and tradition. Why do we need rules?

- Because there is an inherent conflict of interests between profits and wages.
- Because the power of management and labour has to be restrained and balanced.
- Because in industrial situations justice cannot be specified and made to fit all circumstances.
- Because there is no absolute answer to the question – 'what is a fair day's pay for a fair day's work (FDP for a FDW)?'
- Because the wider society needs to be protected from industrial conflict.

There are no right answers to these issues, and they're only solutions that fit particular national circumstances and which will change over time. Labour regulation is a system constantly adjusting to circumstance. At the political level, regulation is guided by political beliefs about the nature of a 'free mar-ket', the degree of collectivism in the society, the interpretation of 'equality' and beliefs about the role of government. Regulation systems vary; some use a strong legal framework as against a largely voluntary approach. Some systems are market-orientated, letting the market handle wage pricing and labour distribution issues. Some are protective of employee rights, making it harder for employers to dismiss workers. And, it is of importance to realise that in most cases the government itself is an employer and has a vested inter-est in the regulatory system. These are essentially political dimensions. How-ever, irrespective of political leanings, all governments are concerns about those aspects of labour regulation which impact upon the economy, namely:

- a rate of wage inflation;
- a level ofproductivity;
- a degree of industrial peace;
- an environment that is either conducive to or detrimental to investment and development.

Rampant price inflation driven by wage demands, low productivity and con-stant disruption are not conducive to investment. The big issues of a regulatory

THE WIDER PERSPECTIVE

system that impact on these concerns are regulating unions and collective bargaining, specifying and limiting strike action. Recognition of unions and the status of collective bargaining are key elements of labour regulation. The objectives of regulation include:

- regulating strike behaviour;
- minimum hours of work;
- employment protection;
- controlling wage inflation.

Many hospitality industries, especially those in large cities, operate in a unionised environment, which makes the regulatory system crucial to daily life. Countries with highly legalised frameworks often means that union agreements are essential operating formats.

If we look at regulation from a human resource perspective, the issues being addressed are always the same.

- Who should be employed? (the discrimination issues)
- What is a FDP for a FDW? (the equality issues)
- How should conflicts within industry be resolved? (the justice issues)
- How can the value of money be retained? (the inflation and productivity issue)
- How much legitimate conflict can a system stand before it discourages investment? (the development issue)

In our original statement we argued that, notwithstanding international circumstances, local dimensions really matter; it can been seen that the daily practice of human resource management is guided by the wider system of labour regulation. The effect of this is that global HRM policies have to be in line with national regulation. They are national norms and traditions concerning employment and pay, and these have to be respected by global corporations because they are often reflected in the regulations themselves. What is possible in one country is forbidden in another. An example of this would be immigration policies which vary from country to country and over time. Whatever the policy is, it is always important to the hospitality industry because of the need for immigrant labour. Two other areas that are usually outside the direct scope of national regulation are international salaries and human resource development.

Cross-border transfer; the benefits issue

One of the most important issues for hospitality is to be able to move people, particularly managers and skilled workers, across national borders. The problems of cross-border recruitment and transfers are:

- that the same job is valued differently in each country;
- that currency differences mean that things are valued differently;

MANAGING IN AN INTERNATIONAL ENVIRONMENT   193

- that the cost of living varies from country to country;
- how can continuous aspects of employment like pay and pensions be managed?

No one wants to worse off through moving to another country, nor do they want to lose any benefits they have already accrued. Simply adjusting salaries will not suffice, because there are differences in the cost of living to be taken into consideration. What assists global HRM in these problems is the indexation of salaries and cost of living indices. Indexation was introduced in Chapter 16; here we broaden the technique.

Cost of living indices are derived from a shopping basket of items that are significant to living that country. Indexation is simply a matter of choosing a base line country and making both salaries and cost of living equal 100. To illustrate a simplistic example, using fictitious figures may help.

The normal practice is to use one year as the base year (= 100) and let all other years be expressed as a percentage of that base year. This combined with the salary of *one occupation* as the base (= 100) and express all other values of pay against the base. If the occupation of a hotel food and beverage manager in Brussels is set as 100, then the same job in other countries can be compared and changes over time revealed.

Base year 2014 = 100; Base location, Brussels; Occupation, Food and Beverage Manager

	2014	2015	2016	2017	2018
Brussels	100	120	120	130	130
London	120	125	130	145	160

When combined with cost of living indices, it is a useful tool in managing employee transfers across borders. Both types of indexation can be usefully combined to give a clearer picture on what a move would mean to an individual. It is a strategic planning tool where the real value is when the surveyor is more interested in the rate of change than in comparing the absolute value.

Indigenous labour and immigration

The starting point of HRM policies is usually 'how do we get people to work in hospitality?' In answering that question, many countries are confronted with two important options; the issues surrounding immigration – that is importing labour from other countries and its corollary developing the indigenous workforce. Pressure often comes directly from governments. Nationalisation, employment policies and programmes are the product of specific political philosophies – and policy and programme objectives are shaped by

194 THE WIDER PERSPECTIVE

those philosophies. Although policies are generic in content, the intention is often to influence specific industries and occupations. In this respect, hospitality is often a target, and nationally oriented employment programmes are inserted within the development process. Although such policies – often called nationalisation programmes – come in different forms depending on their aims and motives, they are, in practice, always about encouraging the indigenous population to take up jobs in the economy and about entreating employers to cooperate in this process by offering training and opportunity to locals. This involves human resource management. Such policies are usually an intervention in labour market functioning aimed at redressing some form of imbalance in the labour market. A common issue is the desire to substitute indigenous workers for expatriate or imported labour. The paradox of needing but not wanting imported labour often creates tension between the needs of the hospitality industry and public policy.

Furthermore, such policies can be problematic simply because they are an intervention in labour market functioning and they raise issues of national identity – who is a national? It is not difficult to see how such policies create problems for hospitality diversity policies. All of this before we get to the cultural issues. Common issues that have to be confronted by local HR managers in relation to both imported and indigenous labour include:

- service work may not be compatible with national culture;
- insufficient financial incentive;
- there may be status and political issues in working in a multicultural environment;
- the serving of alcohol.

These issues are of equal significance when it comes to importing labour from another country. What sits at the back of both immigration and nationalisation policies is the capacity of the hospitality industry to train and develop its own staff. This is a key role for HRM.

Human resource development

Both issues of cross-border transfers and the need for imported labour draw human resource development to the fore. Any discussion of human resource development in hospitality has, firstly, to recognise the value of vocational education in this task; it makes a conspicuous contribution. Hotel and catering schools at craft and managerial levels provide a foundation for in-house development. Secondly, as has been argued in the economic chapters, many skills are easily acquired, which means that the training can be achieved through in-house coaching. Thirdly, that service skills are, to an extent, immune from far-reaching technological change means that the basic manual and social skills will always be necessary. In these circumstances, hospitality has a responsibility to enhance basic skills then develop those particular skills that are required by organisational policy. For any development to be effective and professional it needs:

- to be organised;
- to have well-publicised criteria for recruitment and promotion;
- be incentivised;
- recognise its multicultural context but also;
- be sensitive to the national culture.

A strong development and training scheme needs a clear statement of its purposes and above all *it has to be managed*. The very existence of training opportunities is itself an incentive to personal development.

By its very nature, hospitality is good at handling international perspectives whether this is cross-border transfers and immigration or nationalisation policies. The keys to success are having systems that monitor comparative benefits and above all local HRM management that understands local market conditions and national regulation.

When in Rome?

To a very large extent, yes. Local customs and practice are to be ignored at your peril. Do as the locals do, but corporate HRM with its specified standards on manning, recruitment and training are the essential background framework. Local HRM has to apply corporate standards within a national regulatory framework, so it always has one eye on what is permitted by national law. However, even with corporate chains it is worth remembering that the local labour market has never heard of your strategy; markets have a life of their own.

PART

VI **Development and careers**

CHAPTER

22 Development and careers

This chapter builds upon Chapters 1 and 2, and like them addresses you as an individual and as a manager. The hope is to convince you that careers in hospitality are not just devised by organisations but that they have a structure that can be dictated by you, providing you are open to learning. The hospitality industry offers so many different opportunities and paths and contains such a realm of knowledge, which often spreads beyond its industry borders. We emphasise here that industry-specific skills and knowledge like those of hospitality are not too distant from generic management. The fundamental quality of leadership is always the same. Hospitality managers may speak several languages, but the intrinsic merit of that capability becomes devalued if they can't make a decent decision in any of them! Decision-making and the judgement that lies behind it are the essential qualities of management in any industry. They overlap and must be recognised by the individual manager. Perhaps the most important thing to learn when you start out on a career is that competence is a starting point; it is not an end in itself. Growing means going beyond being capable at a task but having the ability to learn new knowledge.

Chapter objectives

- to appreciate the strategic choices implicit in a career in hospitality;
- to understand basic models of learning by experience;
- to understand that mobility is a vehicle for career development.

The hospitality context

The model in Chapter 12 is a true depiction of the platform on which careers are built, but it lacks one component – the route to entrepreneurship. It is a big omission but one which is forgivable given that this route has so many exit points from the model. Small-scale hospitality ventures do not need large inputs of capital; consequently, many people who have acquired enough skills jump into business. The model, however, is right in showing the influence of social and unsocial hours on careers. There is a clear drift towards working more social hours where there is a market for the same skill set. Again, it is worth emphasising that the vastness of the hospitality industry is something that needs to be comprehended as part of an individual's thinking at an early stage of career development. For a professional manager in the industry, full-time vocational training is the best start for a career. However, thereafter the issue that arises is: can a career be best developed on the lines of the bureaucratic model – that is, by climbing a company ladder or by self-directing a career using the labour market? Both modes of career development are evident in the industry. Hospitality is not immune from the changes in business and technology which have changed career paths, bringing new emphasis to old jobs and creating new ones. Management has become more professional and more specialist whilst at the same time layers of management have been removed and supervision more empowered. The business world has taught managers how to manage from a distance using targets and subcontractors. These changes alter career ladders. The world of generic business and management knowledge is a clear way forward to a hospitality career, but it also alters the way management is constructed so that the traditional operations are, to an extent, detached from the business side of the organisation.

Models of learning by experience

Once you have achieved a formal education in hospitality, there is still a lot to learn. It is very easy to talk of 'getting experience', but this in itself does not guarantee knowledge accumulation. It is not an automatic process. Learning is a mindful task requiring personal objectives and reflection. Three ways of looking at personal development are helpful. The first is the additive model:

- people accumulate skills and knowledge as they go from job to job. Each job adds to their sum of knowledge. This model is related to ideas of human capital.

This model suggests a planned period in different hospitality roles – waiting, cooking, housekeeping, accounts etc. in order to accumulate not only a set of different skills but, most importantly, an overview of the system that all the roles relate to. This last point is crucial. In Chapter 2 we emphasised the need for contextual knowledge, which is knowing the big picture whatever role you have.

The second model is the development model. This does not contradict the additive model but adds a psychological dimension:

- people learn by the differences in skills and knowledge that they find when they start a new job. This model is related to ideas about personal growth and handling authority.

DEVELOPMENT AND CAREERS   201

In effect, this model suggests that you learn by thinking about the differences between your new job and the last one. Being confronted by new issues, new problems and having to get hold of new information is in itself a learning process, but when contrasted with what you knew before it expands your understanding of contextual variables.

The third model is the responsibility model:

- it increases the number of contexts, so people are managing in different circumstances and making decisions with greater consequences of error, moving from tactical to strategic decisions.

This model essentially looks at decision-making and suggests that experience at different levels as well as decision-making based on responsibility is a route to personal growth. So in planning a managerial career there are choices to be made around decision-making development. In evaluating the possibility of a new managerial role, questions can be asked: will I face new types of problems? Will I have more responsibility and have authority over more people and assets? Will my thinking become more long term?

In a sense this model poses the question; do I go for something I know I can do or challenge myself with something bigger or different? This kind of assessment is essential in career planning, and it applies to both organisation career planning and that done by personal mobility.

If you look at the scope of what we call the hospitality industry, we see a vast range of establishments: hotels, restaurants, bars, cafes, industrial and hospital catering, conference organisation, cruise ships, airlines and general facilities and many more, but what they have in common is two essentials: managerial skill and entrepreneurship. So much knowledge and many of the technical and managerial skills are common to a huge variety of tasks across a range of establishments. Furthermore, hospitality is constantly developing through entrepreneurship. Can hospitality management be summed up? Well, one thing a professional hospitality manager is good at is managing complexity in real time. There is an immediacy about hospitality that breeds this capability. This is an asset to be appreciated.

Hospitality and the generic business world

They are not far apart. What is required is the development of generic competencies, such as intellectual competencies, as illustrated below.

> *Planning and causal thinking.* When faced with an opportunity or problem, look at implications, consequences and alternatives. Use 'if-then' scenarios and make strategies.
>
> *Information seeking.* Push for more information to refute ambiguity, to clarify and to probe situations with questions.
>
> *Conceptualisation and synthesis.* Possibly the hardest of all managerial skills is to understand how the parts fit with the whole, in being able to

202 DEVELOPMENT AND CAREERS

identify what is important, use analogies to explain situations and make decisions from fragmented information – *synthesis is as crucial a skill as analysis.*

What is development at a personal level?

The process of self-development begins with recognition that you are responsible for your own knowledge. This is true whether you are studying at an education establishment or developing a career in industry. At any stage in your career, the built technical knowledge grafts onto a personal managerial skill that you have developed for yourself. The guidelines for creating your personal capacity are acknowledging what development is about.

- It is about taking responsibility for your own learning.
- It is about being open to learning new knowledge.
- It is about learning to take responsibility.
- It is about learning to be comfortable in *handling your own managerial authority.*
- It is about learning how to make decisions when there is *incomplete information and uncertainty.*
- It is about feeling competent and projecting competence so that others have confidence in you.

Further reading

Ladkin, A. and Riley, M. (1996) 'Mobility and structure in the career paths of UK hotel managers: a labour market hybrid of the bureaucratic model?' *Tourism Management*, 17, 6: 443–452.

Why read this? This is an authentic portrait of careers in hotels which shows that, at one time, traditional career patterns and values still dominated the industry. This may have changed. The study shows how mobility is used to create careers and which skills lead to what outcomes. It is the clearest picture we have.

Bibliography and further reading

The hospitality context

Alpert, W.T. (1986) *The Minimum Wage in the Restaurant Industry*, London: Praeger.

Brotherton, B. and Wood, R.C. (Eds.) (2008) *The Handbook of Hospitality Management*, New York: Sage.

Brown, D. and McIntosh, S. (2000) 'Job satisfaction and labour turnover in the retail and hotel sectors', in W. Salverda, C. Lucifora and B. Nolan (Eds.) *Policy Measures for Low-Wage Employment in Europe*, Cheltenham: Edward Elgar, pp. 218–237.

Riley, M. (1984) 'Hotels and group identity', *International Journal of Tourism Management*, 5, 2: 102–109.

Riley, M. (1992) 'Labour utilization and collective agreements: an international comparison', *International Journal of Contemporary Hospitality Management*, 4, 4: 21–23.

Riley, M., Ladkin, A. and Szivas, E. (2002) *Tourism Employment: Analysis and Planning*, Clevedon: Channel View Publications.

Wood, R.C. (2018) *Strategic Questions in Food and Beverage Management*, 2nd ed. London: Routledge.

Motivation fundamentals

Herzber, F. (1966) *Work and the Nature of Man*, Chicago: World Publishing Company.

Maslow, A.H. (1943) 'A theory of human motivation', *Psychological Review*, 50: 370–396.

Snyder, R.A. and Williams, R.R. (1982) 'Self theory: an integrative theory of workmotivation', *Journal of Occupational Psychology*, 55, 4: 257–267.

Management and organisational knowledge

Gao, Y. and Riley, M. (2010) 'Knowledge and identity: a review', *International Journal of Management Reviews*, 12, 6: 317–334.

BIBLIOGRAPHY AND FURTHER READING

Hecker, A. (2012) 'Knowledge beyond the individual? Making sense of a notion of collective knowledge in organization theory', *Organization Studies*, 33: 423–448.

Tsoukas, H. (1994) 'Refining common sense: types of knowledge in management studies', *Journal of Management Studies*, 31: 761–780.

Index

Adair, J. 71
administration 137–142; policy guidelines 140
appraisal 154–159; ambiguity 155–156; interview 157–158;.jobs and people 158–159; systems 156–157
architectural organisational knowledge 18
Argyle, M. 153
attitudes 73–80; definitions 74–75; anchors 75–76; characteristics 76; change 79
authority 84–91; and structure 91–92; and communication 93; and power 92–93

Baldwin, J.T. 21
Baker, M. 115, 129
Baron, R.A. 12
Baum, T. 159
bounded rationality 9, 15
Burke, F. 94
bureaucracy 29
bureaucratic model 67
Bushand, S.C. 94

careers 199–202
Carland, J.W. 159
Carland, J.C. 159
Chanda, A. 85
change and learning 61–62
Chua, A. 21
Clark, M.A. 80
commitment 52–62
component organisational knowledge 18
contextual knowledge 18

corporate HRM 181
cross-border transfers 92
cross-substitutions 127

Davidson, M.C.B. 133
decision-making 4–12; process 10–12; rational model 9
demand uncertainty 11
demand fluctuation 14
dispute procedures 176–178
diversity 81–85
D'Netto, B. 85
Doty, D.H. 94

economics of labour 97–107
Eder, R.W. 178
employment interview 163–172; questions 168–172; biases and traps 171–172
empowerment 58–61
Ensley, M.D. 159
Ensley, R.L. 159
equity theory 40
expectancy theory 38

Farouk, S. 21
Ferris, G.R. 173
fluctuating demand 21
forecasting labour supply 120–123
Frank, M. 94
functional flexibility 126–128
Furnham, A. 153

Glascoff, D.W. 94
generic management skills 201–202
grievances 174–178; procedures 176–178; prevention 175–176

INDEX

grievance dilution 49
grievance distortion 49
grievance handling 50–51
group behaviour 63
group process 65–67
group identity 67
group work defined 69
Gronroos, C. 129
leadership in groups 70

Hage, J. 107
Hales, C. 142
Hekman, A. 44
Hertzberg, F. 49
hiring standard 162
hotel and catering labour markets 108–116; high pay 114
HRM policy diversity 84
HRM Strategy 181; vision 181–183; and business 184–189

identity 81–85
immigration 193–194
individual work defined 69
innovation 20–21
internal labour markets 104–107
inter-group relations 68–69
international perspectives 190

job evaluation 147–150
job priorities 29
job satisfaction 52–53
jobs and markets 102–104
Joines, R.C. 21

knowledge context hospitality 13
Key Skills and Attributes (KSAs) 166–168

labour markets 97–107
labour productivity 117–129
labour turnover and stability 130–133
Ladkin, A. 116, 128, 202
Lashley, C. 44
Lepark, D.P. 189
location factor 42
Lockwood, A. 45, 129

management judgement 3–12
management change knowledge 18
management knowledge 17
managing labour supply 123–126
mind-sets 16
models of learning by experience 200–201
motivation 41–44; motivation and society 41; Maslow A. 35

national regulation systems 191–192
negative behaviour 46–51

occupational structure 110
Ogaard, T. 129
Ojasalo, K. 62
organisation 86–94
organisational commitment 56–58
organisational change 59

Park, S. 129
pay management 143–153; pay and leisure 143–144; pay comparisons 144–145
pay systems 145–146
pay structure 146–147
pay surveys 150–153
performance standards 120
personal data 139–140
personal development 13–21, 202
Pierce, J.R. 21
Powell–Perry, J. 45
Pratkanis, A.R. 72
prior knowledge and beliefs 15–16
productivity 117–129; concepts of 118
psychological contract 26–29
psychological inconsistency 47

Rajecki, D.W. 79
recruitment 140–163; and labour turnover 115
Riley, M.J. 45, 62, 80, 116, 128, 129, 189, 202
risk and uncertainty 9
Rousseau, D.M. 31

secular knowledge 16
self-identity 82–88
Shapira, Z. 62

Shen, J. 85
situational knowledge 18
Snell, S.A. 189
skill 103–104, 109–114; model 108; and pay 114
Smith, Adam 104
Snyder and Williams 37
Social Identity Theory 82
stability Index 131–132
supply curve 101
Szivas, E. 116, 138, 189

technical knowledge 18
Timo, N. 133
types of commitment 55–56
types of technological change 16
types of knowledge 18
Turner, M.E. 72

Wang, Y. 136
Wilkie, E. 80
Williams, A. 129
Wood, R.C. 80